VISION OF CHRIST

Stephen Kaung

ISBN: 978-1-942521-58-7

Available from:

Christian Testimony Ministry
4424 Huguenot Road
Richmond, Virginia 23235

www.christiantestimonyministry.com

Printed in USA

PREFACE

"Where there is no vision the people cast off restraint." Proverbs 29:18

Today, more than ever, it is most important that the Lord's people have vision because "without vision, the people perish." Especially as we are living in the last of the last days we need to have a new, fresh and living vision of our Lord Jesus. In the last book of the Bible, The Revelation, we find a series of visions concerning our Lord Jesus in relation to the last days.

During 1978, in Richmond, Virginia, Stephen Kaung shared a series of messages on these seven visions found in the book of Revelation. These spoken messages have been transcribed into this book. The spoken form has been preserved and only necessary editing done for clarity.

Unless otherwise indicated,
Scripture quotations are from
The New Translation by J. N. Darby

CONTENTS

VISION OF CHRIST

Proverbs 29:18 Where there is no vision the people cast off restraint.

Revelation 1:1-3 Revelation of Jesus Christ, which God gave to him, to shew to his bondmen what must shortly take place; and he signified it, sending by his angel to his bondman John, who testified the word of God, and the testimony of Jesus Christ, all things that he saw. Blessed is he that reads, and they that hear the words of the prophecy, and keep the things written in it; for the time is near.

Revelation 1:9-20 I John, your brother and fellow-partaker in the tribulation and kingdom and patience, in Jesus, was in the island called Patmos, for the word of God, and for the testimony of Jesus. I became in the Spirit on the Lord's day, and I heard behind me a great voice as of a trumpet, saying, What thou seest write in a book, and send to the seven assemblies; to Ephesus, and to Smyrna, and to Pergamos, and to Thyatira, and to Sardis, and to Philadelphia, and to Laodicea. And I turned back to see the voice which spoke with me; and having turned, I saw seven golden lamps, and in the midst of the seven lamps one like the Son of man clothed with a garment reaching to the feet, and girt about at the breasts with a golden girdle: his head and hair white like white wool, as snow; and his eyes as a flame of fire; and his feet like fine brass, as burning in a furnace; and his voice as the voice of many waters; and having in his right hand seven stars; and out of his mouth a sharp two-edged sword going forth; and his countenance as the sun shines in its power. And when I saw him I fell at his feet as dead; and he laid his right hand upon me, saying, Fear not; I am the first and the last, and the living one: and I became dead, and behold, I am living to the ages of ages, and have the keys of death and of hades. Write therefore what thou hast seen, and the things that are, and the things that are about to be after these. The mystery of the seven stars which thou hast seen on my right hand, and the seven golden lamps. The seven stars are angels of the seven assemblies; and the seven lamps are seven assemblies.

Shall we pray:

Our Heavenly Father, how we praise and thank Thee for it is Thy good pleasure to reveal Thy Son in us. Therefore, we do come to Thee opening our hearts to Thee and looking to Thy Holy Spirit to once again reveal Thy Son in us that He may fill us and He may be all in all to us. To Thee be the praise and glory. In Thy Precious Name. Amen.

"Where there is no vision the people cast off restraint." In some versions it says, "Where there is no vision the people perish"; or you may put it, where there is no vision the people disintegrate. It is most vital that we have vision, that we see the One who is the eternal purpose of God. We must not only see Him as God's eternal purpose but we must see Him in relation to His people and His church. We need to see Him in relation to the world, in relation to the Jews, in relation to the whole creation, and in relation to God's enemy, Satan and all the powers of darkness. How important it is to see Him; if we do not see Him, we cast off restraint. We will be an undisciplined people. We will be going our own way. If we do not see Him, we perish, the word perish is a very strong word. Let's believe it, if we do not see HIM we perish.

He is our very life. It is by seeing Him that we have hope; we have faith; we have love; we have patience; we have obedience; we have purpose; we have everything. So brothers and sisters, it is of vital importance that we have vision. Of course, vision is not something that we try to visualize as a product of a deranged mind. It will make things worse. A vision is something that God reveals to us. When God reveals, we see. To God it is a revelation given; to us it is a vision seen.

The last book of the Bible is called Revelation. Now of course, we know the whole Bible is the revelation of Jesus Christ. The whole Bible is the revelation of God revealing His Son, Jesus Christ, to us. But the last book of the Bible is especially called The Revelation. In other words, it is in a very special way The Revelation of Jesus Christ, or shall we put it, being the last book, The Consummation of the Revelation of Jesus Christ. The first verse says, "The Revelation of Jesus Christ which God gave to Him to show to His bondmen." Who are His bondmen, His slaves, His love slaves? We are. We who are His redeemed people are His bondmen. Therefore, it is the revelation of Jesus Christ that God gave to Him to show to us. This is what the last book of the Bible is.

In this last book of the Bible, you will see a series of visions of our Lord Jesus, and by the series of visions that John saw, we come to see the revelation of Jesus Christ. Of course, by the grace of God we know our Lord Jesus. We know Him as the crucified One; we know Him as the One who died on the cross in our stead; we know Him as the One whose blood was shed for the remission of our sins; we know Him as the One whose body was broken that we may be joined to God. We know Him as our Savior. We know what He has done for us while He was on earth and on Calvary.

But dear brothers and sisters, our Lord Jesus has been raised from the dead. He has ascended up to heaven. How much do we know Him as the risen Lord in heaven? This is what the book of Revelation is trying to show us. John was a person who knew the Lord very intimately. Of all the disciples of our Lord Jesus, probably there was none who was more intimate in his relationship to the Lord Jesus than the apostle John. He even leaned upon the breast of our Lord Jesus. He knew the Lord. He knew the Lord who walked upon the earth. He followed the Lord; he was the first of the disciples who came to the Lord. He was the only one of the disciples who lingered at the feet of Jesus at the cross. He knew the Lord, the Lord who walked upon the earth, but on the island of Patmos, when he was given a vision of the risen Lord, he was smitten as dead. In other words, he couldn't stand that vision; it was too much for him. It was something he had never fully known before. It had such an affect upon him that he fell down as one dead until he was raised up by the risen Lord.

Now dear brothers and sisters, we know the Lord Jesus who walked upon the earth. We know His death, even His resurrection. We do know what He has done for us, all He has accomplished on earth, but I believe we need to receive a revelation and thus see Him in a different aspect. We need to see Him as the risen Lord in glory.

This is what He is today. Of course, our Lord Jesus is the same yesterday, today and forever. His name is the same. He is the same today in heaven as He was yesterday on earth. So far as His person is concerned, He never changes, but so far as His position, His capacity is concerned, it does change.

While He was on earth, He was the crucified One. Now in heaven, He is the Lord of glory. Today He is the Lord in glory and His relationship with us is a new one, and this is the relationship that we must see. I believe if we see that new relationship, we will fall down as dead. We need to be raised up on to a new ground.

In the book of Revelation, we find a series of the visions of our Lord Jesus. The first vision is recorded in chapter 1. We call it the Patmos vision because John was exiled on the Island of Patmos "for the word of God and for the testimony of Jesus." On the Lord's day he was in the Spirit and heard a voice behind him saying, "Write what thou hast seen and send to the seven churches in Asia." He turned back to look at the voice and he saw. Now what did he see?

He saw One like the Son of man in the midst of the seven golden lampstands. The seven golden lampstands represent the seven churches in Asia because this is explained in the last verse of the first chapter of Revelation. Of course, there were more than seven churches in Asia at that time. Asia is not Asia as a continent, it is Asia as a Roman Province: Asia Minor. If we look at the book of Colossians, we find that Paul mentioned there was a church at Colosse which is in Asia; also the church in Hierapolis is in Asia. But here you will find the Holy Spirit chose seven churches in Asia. Why? Because they represent the church of God throughout the dispensation of grace.

SEVEN CHURCHES, SEVEN GOLDEN LAMPSTANDS

These seven churches are on earth but the Lord Jesus, the One in the midst of the seven golden lampstands, is the Lord in heaven. Here you will find the Lord in heaven, yet the church on earth. In other words, the first vision shows us the relationship between the risen Lord and His church on earth. And what is that relationship? It is a dual relationship. The risen

Lord is shown here, on the one hand, as the glorious Head, the Head of the body which is the church, and on the other hand, as the great High Priest ministering in the heavenly sanctuary. On the one side, we see the church which is His body, the fulness of Him that fills all and in all; and on the other side, we see the church, the true sanctuary, in which Christ as the High Priest ministers. Today, the Lord Jesus to us is the glorious Head; today, the Lord Jesus to us is the High Priest. We need to know Him in these two aspects, and this is the Patmos vision.

First of all, you will find the seven golden lampstands serve as a background, and One like the Son of man serves as the foreground. I think this is something we need to always remember. The church only serves as a background; at the front must be Christ. We cannot reverse that order. It is true that the church is very important in God's heart, and yet it is a background. It is Christ who is at the front. We must see Him, and in seeing Him, we can see the church.

John saw One like the Son of man. He does not say he saw One the Son of man; he says he saw One like the Son of man. Why? You know, the Son of man, is a name the Lord Jesus used for himself while on earth. He said, "The Son of man does not come to be ministered to but to minister and to give His life a ransom for many." When our Lord Jesus was on earth, He was the Son of man because we are of flesh and blood; there-fore, He took part in flesh and blood. "The Word became flesh and tabernacled among men, full of grace and truth." He was the Son of man; He was one of us. He identified Himself with us in order that He may save us. That is why He is called the Son of man; but here you find the Apostle John saying he saw one like the Son of man. Yes, He is the Son of man, and yet he saw Him as one like the Son of man.

You will find this very expression once in the Old Testament, Daniel 7:13-14.

One like a son of man, and he came up even to the Ancient of days, and they brought him near before him. And there was given him dominion, and glory, and a kingdom, that all peoples, nations, and languages should serve him: his dominion is an everlasting dominion.

Of course, we know the Ancient of Days is God and One like the Son of man is our Lord Jesus, but when Daniel received that vision, Christ had not come into the world; therefore, he saw One like the Son of man. But here you will find John saw Him like the Son of man again. The Lord had already come into this world; He was the Son of man. Why is it John saw Him like the Son of man? It is because He had already ascended up to heaven. In other words, He is more than the Son of man. He is the Son of God as well as the Son of man. His glory is a double glory: the glory that He had with the Father even before the foundation of the world and the glory as the Son of man. He is more than the Son; therefore, He is like the Son of man; and you know, dear brothers and sisters, we need to see Him today as such.

Some people see the Lord Jesus only as the Son of One who is very approachable, One who is very near, One who is one of us, One with whom you can be very familiar, and this is right; He is the Son of man. However, sometimes we can become so familiar with Him, and as the saying goes, "familiarity breeds contempt", that we do not have that reverence which we should give to Him. Then you will find other people who know Him only as the Son of God, the One who is high above, separated from us, transcendent. They only stand in fear and trembling before Him. They do not dare to even approach Him because He is the Son of God. With us, dear brothers and sisters, it should be both. On the one hand, we should see Him as the Son of man who is one of us; we can be very near and very close with Him, having a friendship with Him. Yet on the other hand, we cannot but always stand in awe and reverence because He is the Son of God. This is the balance that we must have today. Today among God's people, you will find two extremes. Some always stand in awe of Him and dare not approach Him. They give Him all the reverence that is His due. Then there are some that become so familiar with Him that there is no reverence, and because of that, they can become careless. Today the relationship of our Lord Jesus with the church is as the Son of man and the Son of God. This is our relationship with Him.

Next you will find John saw One clothed with a garment reaching to the feet. You know, garment in the Scripture always signifies our conduct, our behavior, our manner of life. It is like a garment put upon us. Now of course, we have no righteousness of our own. The prophet Isaiah said, "All our righteousness is as filthy rags." It cannot cover our nakedness; therefore, we cannot stand before God. Here you will find the Lord Jesus as the glorious Head in heaven who is clothed with a garment reaching to the feet; that is to say, He is full of righteousness. Our Lord Jesus is the righteous One. It is because as the righteous One, He is able to be our substitute: the just dying for the unjust.

Him who knew not sin he has made sin for us, that we might become God's righteousness in him. (2 Corinthians 5:21)

So dear brothers and sisters, today how can we stand before God? Our standing before God is because we are clothed with Christ, our righteousness.

As a young man, John Bunyan (who wrote Pilgrim's Progress) was convicted of sins from time to time and tried to reform himself, but never succeeded. Once he was walking in the field, thinking about this matter: How can a man be justified before God? Suddenly, he heard as a voice saying to him, "My righteousness is in heaven." This revelation had a tremendous affect upon him.

Our brother, Watchman Nee, once said we may change but our righteousness never changes. Do we change? Certainly! From morning to evening we change, we don't know how many changes. Because we change, does it affect our standing before God? Suppose in the morning after a good night's sleep you get up and feel good. You come to the Lord feeling you have every right to approach Him and to have a good time with the Lord. But then you go out to work, you begin to find some difficult people and difficult problems, and towards the evening you are rather beaten. You come home and before you go to bed, you try to pray again. As you try to pray, does it affect your standing before God? Because you are not as fresh as in the morning, your approach to God seems to be affected. Suppose during the day, you lose your temper. Do you dare to pray? Do you think you must have five minutes to blame yourself before you pray? Does your change affect your standing before God? How do you stand before God? Do you stand before God on your own righteousness? Brothers and sisters, you are clothed with Christ as your righteousness and He is the only reason for which you can stand before God. Whether you are good or bad does not affect your standing. If you are good, it does not add anything to your standing before God. If you are bad, it does not take anything away from your standing before God because you are clothed with Christ, your righteousness. We may change but our righteousness never changes. Christ, our righteousness, is our ONLY standing before God. Whether you feel good or bad, if you see Christ, your righteousness, you are able to stand, to approach God.

Does it mean to say we can be bad? Not at all. In 1 John 2:1, we are told, "My children, these things I write to you in order that you may not sin." Then it also says, "And if any one sin, we have an advocate with the Father, Jesus Christ the righteous; and he is the propitiation for our sins; but not for ours alone, but also for the whole world." What is the meaning there? On the one hand, it says that we may not sin, that is how we should be. On the other hand, if we sin, what should we do? Is our relationship with God cut because we sin? Is it cut off for a day or an hour? No. It says we have an advocate with the Father. The word advocate is the same word translated comforter in the Gospel of John, paracletos. We have our Paracletos with the Father. Now, who is this? Jesus, the righteous. In other words, if we sin, let's confess our sins.

If we confess our sins, he is faithful and righteous to forgive us our sins, and cleanse us from all unrighteousness. (1 John 1:9)

If we sin, we confess and we find Christ, our righteousness, is always there; therefore, our fellowship with the Father need not be interrupted. Brothers and sisters, we need to see that we are clothed with Christ, our righteousness and this is our only standing. Even if we should fall, He hasn't fallen.

Our Head is full of righteousness and because He is full of righteousness, He expects His body to be full of righteousness. His body is the fulness of Him who fills all in all. To put it in another way, what the Head is, that is what the body must be. It is true, on the one hand, we are clothed with Christ as our righteousness; but there is more. As Christ is righteous, He expects us also to practice righteousness. He who practices righteousness is a child of God. He who practices sin is a child of the devil. So you will find it is more than just a matter of standing before God, it is also a matter of state or condition. Our standing never changes because it is Christ, our righteousness. But how about our state? How about our condition? Are we full of righteousness as our Head is full of righteousness? As the Head, He demands that His body be filled with righteousness, practical righteousness.

We must be clothed with two garments, not one. Psalm 45 is about the king and queen; the king, of course, is the Lord and the queen is the church. There you will find the queen is ready, ready for the king. How is she ready? She is clothed with a garment of wrought gold and over and above that garment is a raiment of embroidery. The garment of wrought gold is Christ, our righteousness; but after we are clothed with Christ, our righteousness, then the Holy Spirit will embroider in us the beauty of the Lord. When the Holy Spirit embroiders into our life, even into our very fiber, the characters of Christ, they become the raiment of embroidery. In Revelation 19, this is called "the righteousnesses of the saints."

Let us rejoice and exult, and give him glory; for the marriage of the Lamb is come, and his wife has made herself ready. And it was given to her that she should be clothed in fine linen, bright and pure; for the fine linen is the righteousnesses of the saints. (Revelation 19:7-8)

This is practical righteousness. Brothers and sisters, we must allow the Holy Spirit to embroider, weave, knit or stitch Christ into our very life so that the characters of Christ may become our characters in our words, deeds, manners, looks, relationships, even in our whole conduct and behavior. It will be all of Christ and, when that is true, it is called the righteousnesses of the saints.

Christ as the glorious Head is full of righteousness. Whatever He does is right in the sight of God. Whatever He says is right in the sight of God. In all His relationships with man, He is right in the sight of God. In His relationship with His family, He is right in the sight of God. In His relationships with His disciples, He is right in the sight of God. In His relationship with His enemies, He is right in the sight of God. You will find that every word, deed, action, reaction, look and manner of our Lord Jesus is right in the sight of God. This is what it ought to be. Brothers and sisters, the Head demands nothing less than that of His church.

We may think that because we are clothed with Christ, our righteousness, He is our standing before God, therefore, we can be negligent or careless in our walk. We think that, after all, Christ is our righteousness; but there is the other side: "He who practices righteousness is of God" because God is righteous. Are we really righteous? Do we live a righteous life? In our relationships, in the work of our hands, in our manner of life, in our words, in our actions and reactions, is it Christ or is it us? The glorious Head is full of righteousness and the body is the fulness of Him who fills all in all.

No wonder John fell down as one dead when he saw this. Before Christ the righteous One, he sensed his own unrighteousness. Brothers and sisters, we need to see that the glorious Head demands of us a righteousness that is like His. Who can stand up? Thank God, He who demands this of us is able to supply our every need as He is our great High Priest who ministers in the heavenly sanctuary. Now what is a high priest? What is his work? A high priest is one who ministers. In Hebrews 7:25, we are told that:

Our Lord Jesus ever liveth to make intercession for us and is able to save those who come to God by Him to the uttermost.

He knows we have no righteousness of our own. If we try to be righteous, we cannot do it; but brothers and sisters, He is our High Priest. He is here waiting to supply us with such righteousness. Oh, how we need to come to Him and say: "Lord, I cannot do it; but You can. I cast myself upon You. You carry me through." Then you will find you can act or react in the way that He would act or react because it is not you; it is Christ in you, the hope of glory. This is the relationship of our Lord Jesus today with His church. He wants us to be what He is and He is available to us to make it real if only we come to Him.

Now this is just the first description of our Lord Jesus, full of righteousness. We cannot go into every one of them but I will just mention them. You will find He has a golden girdle around his breasts which shows that He is full of divine love and compassion, and because He is full of love and compassion, He demands that His church be full of divine love. Unless we acknowledge that we cannot love, we will not be able to love as He loves. If we think we can love, we will be found wanting in love. How often, because of His love for us, He allows us to be put in a situation where our love is tested beyond our measure so that we may find we just do not have love. It is just at that point that we know Him as our High Priest who will love in and through us.

"His head and hair white like white wool, as snow." In other words, He is full of divine wisdom. He demands His church to be full of wisdom; but do we have wisdom? If we boast that we do, our wisdom is from beneath; and when we have that earthly wisdom, it will bring strife and emulation.

But the wisdom from above first is pure, then peaceful, gentle, yielding, full of mercy and good fruits, unquestioning, unfeigned. (James 3:17)

This wisdom from above is not hard, harsh or rigid.

"His eyes as a flame of fire." He is full of spiritual discernment. He expects us to have discernment, but do we have it? As you grow, have experiences and observe some things in the world, you do have a certain amount of discernment; but that kind only makes you critical. It is spiritual discernment that enables you to minister and build, not destroy.

"And his feet like fine brass, as burning in a furnace." He is full of divine judgment, and He expects His church to be full of judgment. He does not want us to be willy-nilly and say, "Oh, everything is all right." What He has discerned,

He tramples upon if it is not of Him. There needs to be divine judgment and He will supply that.

"And his voice as the voice of many waters." He is full of majesty and authority, spiritual authority.

"And in his right hand seven stars." He is full of strength to support responsibility.

"And out of his mouth a sharp two-edged sword going forth." He is full of Power, dividing and penetrating.

"And his countenance as the sun shines in its power." You know your face reveals your health. We say "rosy cheeks" and it means you are very healthy, and if you are sick, we say "pale face." In other words, there is such inward beauty and healthiness in Him that it expresses itself outwardly. Do you know that is what He expects of His church, to be full of inward beauty. This beauty of Christ should be seen.

Oh brothers and sisters, as you go through every item of His life, you will fall down as one dead. You will say: "Lord, I don't have this. I don't have that. I think I have it, but it is a counterfeit. It doesn't work." You just have to say, "Lord, you are the Head, we are the body and what a difference there is."

Yet thank God, His hand is upon us and He will raise us up out of death into resurrection and say: "Fear not; I am the first and the last, and the living one: and I became dead and behold, I am living to the ages of ages and have the keys of death and of hades." In other words, He, as the High Priest, will supply all of these to us. This vision that John saw becomes a trust, the testimony of Jesus. This vision is the light of the lampstand. We need to see; then we have the light. On one side, it is a tremendous privilege, but on the other, it is a great responsibility. Today we must see Christ as the glorious Head in such a way that it will bring us to a sense of inadequacy, a real sensing of our incompetency. I believe God wants us to see Christ as the High Priest who ever liveth to make intercession, able to save us to the uttermost. If we can see this, then we have a testimony to bear in this world.

Shall we pray:

Our Heavenly Father, we do praise and thank Thee because Thou art the One who reveals Thyself. It is Thy good pleasure to reveal Thy Son in us. Thou dost desire us to see the Patmos vision just as Thou showed to John, Thy servant. We do pray that by Thy Holy Spirit we may see the risen One as the glorious Head of the church, full of righteousness, full of love, full of wisdom, full of discernment, full of judgment, full of authority, power, strength, full of beauty. Oh, that we may see Thee, Head over all things to the church which is Your body, the fulness of Him who fills all in all and we do pray we may see Thee as the High Priest. We thank Thee this is Your ministry today towards us in heaven. Oh, how effective, how real, how living, how available is Your ministry today that we may avail ourselves of Your ministry and thus be brought to the place where we may bear Your testimony on this earth. To Thee be all the glory. In the Name of our Lord Jesus. Amen.

VISION OF THE THRONE OF GOD AND OF THE LAMB

Revelation 4:1-5 After these things I saw, and behold, a door opened in heaven, and the first voice which I heard as of a trumpet speaking with me, saying, Come up here, and I will show thee the things which must take place after these things. Immediately I became in the Spirit; and behold, a throne stood in the heaven, and upon the throne one sitting, and he that was sitting like in appearance to a stone of jasper and a sardius, and a rainbow round the throne like in appearance to an emerald. And round the throne twenty-four thrones, and on the thrones twenty-four elders sitting, clothed with white garments; and on their heads golden crowns. And out of the throne go forth lightnings, and voices, and thunders; and seven lamps of fire, burning before the throne, which are the seven Spirits of God.

Revelation 5:1-10 And I saw on the right hand of him that sat upon the throne a book, written within and on the back, sealed with seven seals.

And I saw a strong angel proclaiming with a loud voice, Who is worthy to open the book, and to break its seals? And no one was able in the heaven, or upon the earth, or underneath the earth, to open the book, or to regard it. And I wept much because no one had been found worthy to open the book nor to regard it. And one of the elders says to me, Do not weep. Behold, the lion which is of the tribe of Juda, the root of David, has overcome so as to open the book, and its seven seals. And I saw in the midst of the throne and of the four living creatures, and in the midst of the elders, a Lamb standing, as slain, having seven horns and seven eyes, which are the seven Spirits of God which are sent into all the earth: and it came and took it out of the right hand of him that sat upon the throne. And when it took the book, the four living creatures and the twenty-four elders fell before the Lamb, having each a harp and golden bowls full of incenses, which are the prayers of the saints. And they sing a new song, saying, Thou art worthy to take the book, and to open its seals; because thou hast been slain, and hast redeemed to God, by thy blood, out of every tribe, and tongue and people, and nation, and

*made them to our God kings and priests; and they
shall reign over the earth.*

When we were together last time, we
mentioned that the book of Revelation is the
book of the revelation of Jesus Christ. Actually
nothing really matters but the revelation of Jesus
Christ. If we have the revelation of Jesus Christ,
we have everything. If we do not have the
revelation of Jesus Christ, no matter how much
we have, we have nothing. When God reveals His
Son, then we see Him. To God it is revelation, to
us it is vision.

Now we would like to come to the second
vision of our Lord Jesus in the book of
Revelation, chapters 4 and 5. John said that the
heaven was opened and he was in the Spirit and
there he saw something. He said he saw a throne
in heaven. Now dear brothers and sisters, if the
heaven is opened to us, if we are in the spirit of
rapture, what will we see in heaven? We will see
in heaven the throne, the throne of God. On
earth, we see the cross; but in heaven, we see the
throne. If we do not see the throne in heaven, it
is because the heaven is not open to us. If we do

not see the throne in heaven, it is because we are not in the spirit of rapture. Whoever is in the spirit of rapture and has the heaven really opened to him has access to heaven. He can see through into heaven, and if he does, he will invariably see one thing there, the throne of God. No matter what happens on earth, there is one thing that never changes, and it is the throne of God. When in that vision, John saw the throne in heaven, he saw it undisturbed. Yes, in history there was the rebelling of the archangel. In history, there was the fall of man. But whether there was the rebelling of the archangel or the fall of man, it didn't change anything in heaven. The throne of God is still there. It never changes!

"Thy throne, O God, is for ever and ever; a scepter of uprightness is the scepter of thy kingdom." The throne of God is in heaven. On earth, there is confusion. On earth, many things have happened; but in heaven, the throne is set forever and forever. Righteousness and justice are the foundation of the throne of God. Lovingkindness and truth go before His face. The throne of God is there in heaven and heaven rules over the earth. No matter what happens on earth, heaven is ruling and overlooking upon the things of the earth.

Dear brothers and sisters, how we need to see the throne of God. Oftentimes, we are surrounded by things that happen on this earth. We are occupied with those things that confront us in our immediate circumstances. Also, we are disturbed by the things that are going on in our city, state, country and in the world. When we are occupied by these things, we lose sight of the throne of God. Sometimes, we seem to think that evil has its way. It seems as if Satan is truly the ruler of this earth, but dear brothers and sisters, this is the time we need to have an open heaven. We need to be in the spirit of rapture. If we see the throne of God, we will rise above our circumstances. We will be delivered from all confusion, disturbance, disappointment and discouragement and we will be joined to that throne; and because of that, we will be able to be as kings and priests unto God. THE THRONE OF GOD, all power and authority is there. Everything proceeds from that throne. Nothing happens on earth that is outside of the power and authority of that throne. THIS IS SOMETHING WE MUST SEE!

We know the One whom John saw sitting upon the throne is our God; but of course, no one can see God. God is a Spirit. What John saw, the One who sits upon the throne, was One like in appearance to a stone of jasper and a sardius. In other words, John did not really see God because He could not be seen, but he received an impression of God and that impression is being presented here to us in colors. Now the color of jasper is blue, like the heavens, and the color of sardius is red. There is a rainbow all around the throne. When we see a rainbow, we usually see it as half a circle, at most. Here, it is a rainbow all around the throne, a full circle. Of course, a rainbow is a blending of all colors, but in that blending of colors, one color stands out, the color of emerald, which is green. So dear brothers and sisters, you see here beautiful colors giving us an impression of the One who sits upon the throne. Blue speaks of being heavenly, red of royalty and green is the color of life; everything of life is in green (green grass). The impression that is given to us is that our God is so heavenly, so majestic, so royal, so full of life; and it is shown to us like a stone. A stone speaks of stability, of permanency; and being precious stones, it gives us the value of it. Our God upon the throne is full of value, stable, like a rock, and He is beautiful, heavenly, royal and full of life.

Now we know that chapter 4 of the book of Revelation is a description of the glory of the Creator; and the glory of the Creator, of course, extends throughout the period of creation. There you will find God on the throne, reigning over His creation, and the whole creation is represented by the four living creatures. The twenty-four elders represent the government of God over His creation. In this vision of God reigning over His creation, there is no interruption, no intermission. From the day of creation onward, there has been no interruption of His reign.

Next you find, "And out of the throne go forth lightnings, and voices, and thunders; and seven lamps of fire, burning before the throne, which are the seven Spirits of God." In other words, the throne of God is very active. It's not that after God created everything, He left it and let creation work out its own way. No! After God created the universe, the creatures, the whole creation, He rules and reigns over it actively. Lightning, thunder, etc., these all describe to us action; it is in the power and energy of the Holy Spirit.

Brothers and sisters, I do want you to get such an impression because we are living in a very difficult time. We are living at the end of the end days. Because we are living in such a time, so many things are happening on earth with such intensity and speed that there is much confusion. If we do not have such a vision of the One who sits upon the throne who is actively reigning over His creation, brothers and sisters, our faith may falter. We may lose hope and our love will get cold. So it is of vital importance that we see the vision of the throne of God. Do not be deceived by what appears to you on earth, but believe what God has revealed to you, that He is on the throne and He does rule and reign over all things.

Even though, in chapter 4, we do not see the whole creation or angelic host singing praises unto God, yet we find they are represented by the four living creatures and the twenty-four elders. These four living creatures cry out day and night, "Holy, holy, holy, Lord God Almighty." The whole creation is praising God the Creator. It never ceases. It is true, when you look into history, the whole creation has entered into vanity and is under the bondage of corruption. The whole creation groans. Yet dear brothers and sisters, if you rise above appearance and get into reality, if you are delivered from time and get into eternity, what will you see? You will see the whole creation, represented by the four living creatures, praising God all of the time, without end, not groaning, but praising. While they are doing that, the twenty-four elders worship God, and they reveal the purpose of creation to us. Why is it the whole creation is praising God? Because God has created them for His own pleasure. The purpose of creation is to please God, to make Him happy and satisfy His heart. The whole creation is not created for itself but for God and His satisfaction. This is the picture we see in Revelation 4, but this is only part of the vision. The other is shown to us in chapter 5.

In chapter 5, it seems that something has happened. We do not get an impression that anything has happened in chapter 4. It seems that since the day of creation, everything goes on according to God's purpose and nothing is really changed; thank God that is so. But when you come to chapter 5, something has happened. In this chapter, the Spirit of God recognized that something had happened to creation, the rebelling of the archangel and the fall of man. After man fell into the hands of Satan, Satan organized this world into a system to resist God. He became the usurper of this world; may I say, he was the squatter. He seemed to occupy God's creation. When chapter 5 opens, John saw "on the right hand of him that sat upon the throne a book, written within and on the back, sealed with seven seals." We know that this book is the title deed of the creation and God holds it. Satan may usurp on this earth, but God has not given up His ownership. Do not think that because Satan seems to occupy this earth and usurp it that he owns it. He does not! The ownership is still in God's hand.

There was the declaration: "And I saw a strong angel proclaiming with a loud voice, Who is worthy to open the book, and to break its seals?" In other words, the ownership is in God's hands but God needs someone to execute His will. God needs someone to bring back to Him the whole creation as it was originally designed. Now that is the problem. It is not with ownership because God never gives up His ownership. The problem is: who is able to take the whole thing back and bring all of creation into subjection to God's purpose? The one who is to do that has to be worthy, HAS TO BE WORTHY.

So the proclamation went out: "Who is worthy to take the book and open the seven seals?" There must have been such suspense. There was no one worthy in heaven or earth or under the earth; and when time began to fly, when there was no answer, when no one came forward, John wept. He wept much. In other words, he thought it was finished, that the whole creation was finished, out of God's hand and in the hand of Satan, that it would not be recovered, would not be released, so he wept much. Then he was comforted by one of the elders who said, "Do not weep, there is One who is worthy." Now who is the worthy One? The Lion of the Tribe of Judah and the root of David. At that moment, John saw. Dear brothers and sisters, John saw One, a Lamb, standing as newly slain and He came forward and took the roll out of the hand of the One who sits upon the throne. He took it and, when He did, the praises burst out from the four living creatures and the elders. They played the harp and they offered the incense, which is the prayers of the saints.

Revelation 5 is a scene of the ascension of our Lord Jesus. In the book of Acts, the Lord led His disciples to Mount Olive and there He was taken up. They saw Him going up and a cloud taking Him. They could not see Him, but they were still looking as the cloud was going up and up. Then two men appeared and said:

Men of Galilee, why do ye stand looking into heaven? This Jesus who has been taken up from you into heaven, shall thus come in the manner in which ye have beheld him going into heaven. (Acts 1:11)

So our Lord Jesus was ascended up to heaven but no one saw the scene of His ascension. What happened when He arrived in heaven? We know He arrived. How do we know? On the day of Pentecost, the Holy Spirit was poured forth. There was the evidence that He had arrived in heaven. He was anointed and the oil came down from the Head to the very skirts of the garment. Nobody saw the scene of His ascension, but here in chapter 5, we are shown that scene. Historically speaking, chapter 5 gives us the scene of the ascension of our Lord Jesus. Why? Because He was there as a lamb newly slain, not slain 2000 years ago, but He was seen as a lamb newly slain. It was only forty days after His resurrection. A LAMB NEWLY SLAIN. When He ascended up to heaven, what happened? He took from God's hand that roll. In other words, He was made the Heir of all things.

You remember Psalm 2:8, "Ask of me, and I will give the nations for an inheritance, and for thy possession the ends of the earth." Here you will find our Lord Jesus is the Heir of all creation. He received the ownership of all creation and now it is up to Him to open the seals, that is, to execute the will of God, to bring all things into subjection to God. He is worthy. Why? Because He has overcome. He has overcome sin. He has overcome the flesh. He has overcome the world. He has overcome Satan, the usurper of this world. In other words, on Calvary's cross, He has won the victory.

THERE ON CALVARY'S CROSS

He bore our sins. "The Lamb of God who takes away the sin of the world." He put away our sins.

THERE ON CALVARY'S CROSS

Our old man was crucified with Him. The flesh was dealt with.

THERE ON CALVARY'S CROSS

The world was crucified. Though the world crucified Him, yet on the cross, He crucified the world.

THERE ON CALVARY'S CROSS

He stripped Satan of his power and made a public show of him in triumph of the cross.

In other words, here you will find this Lamb is the only One in the whole universe who is worthy. Nobody has ever overcome sin. Nobody has ever overcome the flesh. Nobody has ever overcome the world. Nobody has ever overcome Satan.

But here, our Lord Jesus is the Conqueror, and because He has overcome, He has the power to execute the will of God. It is a matter of worthiness and the worthiness is based upon His overcoming. Dear brothers and sisters, our Lord Jesus has already overcome and won the victory on Calvary's cross. He is now crowned with glory and honor. He is made the Heir of all things and He sits at the right hand of God, waiting for His enemies to be His footstool. He will bring everything into subjection unto Christ and, after that is done, then He will give all things back to God (see 1 Corinthians 15:28).

Dear brothers and sisters, the angel declares, "The Lion of the Tribe of Judah has overcome"; but when John saw, he saw the Lamb. The declaration is the Lion, but the vision is the Lamb. You know, the lion and the lamb are two opposites. The lion speaks of majesty, of strength, of power. The lion will instill a sense of fear and awe into us. The lion will devour. The lamb speaks of meekness and lowliness. A lamb will give us an impression of love. A lamb is to be sacrificed. The lion and the lamb, two opposites, are joined together in Christ. The lion power of our Lord Jesus is in His lamb nature. It is the Lamb in the midst of the throne.

It is interesting to note in the Old Testament that, when Solomon built his throne, it was lined with lions. Why? Because lions speak of royalty and majesty. Yet here, the One who sits upon the throne is the Lamb, the Lamb in the midst of the throne. His victory, His power, His overcoming is in His lowliness and meekness. What is lowliness? What is meekness? Philippians 2:6-8 says:

Christ Jesus, who existing in the form of God, counted not the being on an equality with God a thing to be grasped, but emptied himself, taking the form of a servant being made in the likeness of men; and being found in fashion as a man, he humbled himself, becoming obedient, even unto death, yea, the death of the cross.

That is lowliness. That is meekness. Lowliness and meekness mean selflessness. Our Lord Jesus overcame sin, flesh, the world and Satan because of His lamb nature, of His selflessness, of His being willing to empty Himself, of His humbling Himself even unto death. He was obedient to the Father because He sacrificed Himself for the whole world. That is where His strength is, where His victory is.

Chapter 5 is a picture of the glory of the Redeemer. Of course, so far as redemption is concerned, man is in the very center of the redemptive work of God and that is why you will find the twenty-four elders and the four living creatures singing the new song. It is a song of redemption. They sing of how God has redeemed us out of every nation and tribe and tongue and has made us to be kings and priests unto God. What a redemption! But dear brothers and sisters, at this point, the saints begin to pray because the twenty-four elders and the four living creatures offer up incenses which are the prayers of the saints. We who are redeemed must begin to pray right away because, by the prayer of the church, the whole creation is being restored to Christ.

So far as the foundation is concerned, it is already laid, the foundation of victory, Christ has already overcome every force that holds back the creation from God's purpose. Christ has broken all the powers that bind the creation. He has already overcome and now it is left to the church to pray, "Thy kingdom come, Thy will be done on earth as it is in heaven". As the church prays, then the victory of Christ will be executed upon all things until all things are brought into subjection.

In Ephesians 1:23, it says, "Christ the Head over all things to the church which is His body, the fulness of Him who fills all and in all." In other words, we are kings; we are priests. Now do not think that we will be kings and we will be priests in the millennium, the kingdom of God that is to come. No. Brothers and sisters, He has bought us and washed us with His blood and He has made us kings and priests unto God TODAY. In what sense are we kings and priests unto God? In the sense that, being united with Christ, we are priests who will pray and kings who will rule. In other words, the victory of Christ shall bear upon all things through the cooperation of the church. I often say the work of the church today is the "mopping up." The victory is won and we are to go forth to "mop up", to apply the victory of Christ and bring all things into subjection to Christ. That is the tremendous work that is committed to the church. That is why the Lord said, "Whatever you bind on earth shall be bound in heaven and whatever you loose on earth shall be loosed in heaven", kings and priests unto God.

As you read chapter 5, you immediately find the angelic host and all creation begin to sing the anthem of praise. It is as if all creation has been restored, is already restored. Brothers and sisters, when you look into history, you have the past, present and future; but when you look into reality, there is no past or future, it is all present. Therefore, even though it is the ascension of our Lord Jesus, here you will find the whole creation bursts out into praises as if the whole creation has been restored. Historically, we are waiting for the restoration of all things; but spiritually, it is all restored. Every knee has already bowed, every tongue has already confessed that Jesus is Lord. Oh! Wonderful, How wonderful it is!

Dear brothers and sisters, this is the vision God wants us to see concerning our Lord Jesus. If we really see the throne of God, the first affect upon us will be that we submit ourselves to God and His authority. What's the use of talking about the throne of God if we are only thinking in terms of the world knowing His authority! We, ourselves, must first know the throne of God. The throne of God as it sits in heaven must be seated in our HEARTS. If the throne of God is not seated in our hearts, we do not see the throne of God in heaven. The first affect of seeing the throne of God in heaven will be our bowing before God and saying, "Lord, You set Your throne in my heart." If we do this, then out of us will come forth the authority and the power of the throne of God. Do not expect the authority and the power of God's throne to be manifested in and through us if we ourselves have not submitted to His authority.

Who is in the midst of the throne? The Lamb in the midst of the throne. Brothers and sisters, if we desire to be in touch with the throne, we must have the life of the Lamb. In our human mentality, it is very difficult to connect these two things. We cannot connect a lion with a lamb. May I use the following illustration:

You remember, before our Lord was crucified, John and James came with their mother to see Him. (I often laugh at it because it is such maneuvering.) They came to Him and said: "Whatever we want, give it to us. Sign a blank check." The Lord asked, "What do you want?" Their mother said, "Let one of my sons sit on Your right hand and the other on Your left." In other words, throne, authority. The Lord said: "Can you be baptized with the baptism with which I am going to be baptized? Can you drink the cup that I am going to drink?" Without really knowing what they meant, the sons replied "Yes" because they were so anxious for the throne. The Lord said, "Yes, you must; but to sit on My right hand or left is not for Me to give, but the Father."

We cannot connect the throne with baptism. We cannot connect the throne with the cup because, with us, the throne and the baptism and the cup are two opposites. If you are baptized, if you drink the cup, you are at the lowest end. Now if you sit on the throne, you are on a higher end. Dear brothers and sisters, what the Lord is trying to teach us is this, there is the Lamb in the midst of the throne and what He is, He sets as an example for us. If we want to reach the throne, we have to be like lambs, not like lions. Oh, the disciples strove for the throne like lions. They devoured each other. Unless we have the spirit of the lamb manifested in our lives, we are not in the midst of the throne. Our authority, our power is in the Spirit of Christ.

Dear brothers and sisters, may we catch that vision. May we see that the Lord is in the midst of the throne; that God reigns; that our Lord Jesus has already overcome; that He is executing the will of God concerning the whole creation. May we see our part in it.

It is through the church that God will bring all things into subjection and, one day, there will be restoration of all things. In other words, the whole creation will be restored to the original design of God, created for His good pleasure. Praise God. May we see it.

Shall we pray:

Our Heavenly Father, we do pray that, by Thy Holy Spirit, we will be given a vision of Thy Son as the Lamb in the midst of the throne. Oh, may we see that He has overcome. He is the Heir of all things. He is worthy to open the book and He is executing Thy will. There is no question about the outcome. But, Lord, we also ask Thee, as Thou dost show us Thy Son, our Lord Jesus as a Lamb in the midst of the throne, that Thou will teach us the lesson that we need to learn. Oh, that we may be filled with the Spirit of the Lamb that we may be in touch with Thy throne and be given authority and power in working together with Thee for the restoration of all things. To the praise and glory of God. In Thy precious name. Amen.

VISION OF THE LORD JESUS: THE STRONG ANGEL

Revelation 10:1-7 And I saw another strong angel coming down out of the heaven, clothed with a cloud, and the rainbow upon his head, and his countenance as the sun, and his feet as pillars of fire, and having in his hand a little opened book. And he set his right foot on the sea, and the left upon the earth, and cried with a loud voice as a lion roars. And when he cried, the seven thunders uttered their own voices. And when the seven thunders spoke, I was about to write: and I heard a voice out of the heaven saying, Seal the things which the seven thunders have spoken, and write them not. And the angel whom I saw stand on the sea and on the earth lifted up his right hand to the heaven, and swore by him that lives to the ages of ages, who created the heaven and the things that are in it, and the earth and the things that are in it, and the sea and the things that are in it, that there should be no longer delay; but in the days of the voice of the seventh angel, when he is about to sound the trumpet, the mystery of God also shall be completed, as he has made known the glad tidings to his own bondmen the prophets.

The book of Revelation is the revelation of Jesus Christ which God gave to Him to show to us, His bondmen. In other words, in this book God intends to reveal His Son, our Lord Jesus Christ, to us. When God reveals, we see; so to us, it is a vision. Through the revelation of God, we see the Lord Jesus in a new way, in a way that we have never seen before.

In the first vision of our Lord Jesus recorded, in the first chapter of this book, we see Him as One like the son of man in the midst of the seven golden lampstands. Then in Revelation 4 and 5, in the second vision of our Lord Jesus, a Lamb in the midst of the throne. Because of His emptying Himself, humbling Himself, being obedient to the Father, even unto death and the death of the cross, the Lamb is today in the midst of the throne, in the place of authority and power.

In the third vision, we find it is a continuation. Why? Because in the fifth chapter, we see the Lamb in the midst of the throne, receiving a book sealed with seven seals. He received the book because He is worthy. He received the book in order to open the seals. Immediately after the fifth chapter, the Lamb began to open the seals, and when you come to the tenth chapter, all the seven seals have been opened. Here a strong angel is coming down out of heaven. In the fifth chapter, we find the Lamb in the midst of the throne, which depicts the ascension of our Lord Jesus. After He accomplished salvation, He ascended up on high and received the earth as His inheritance from the Father. But here we find the strong angel descending out of heaven.

In chapter 5, it is ascending to heaven. In chapter 10, it is descending out of heaven. In chapter 5, it is the beginning of the restoration of all things to God's purpose. In chapter 10, it is toward the ending of the work of restoring all things to the Father.

We know this strong angel is none other than our Lord Jesus. Now how do we know this? We know by the way this angel is being described. First of all, we find he is called an angel. In the

Old Testament, whenever you find the angel of the Lord, you know that it is referring to the second Person of the Godhead. It is the Lord. So here again in the Revelation, you will find He is called an angel. Why? Because angels are ministering spirits. They are sent by God to serve God's purpose. In one sense, you find our Lord Jesus is sent by the Father to minister to the Father's will. While He was on earth, He said, "The Son can do nothing of himself save whatever he sees the Father doing" (John 5:19). Throughout His life on earth, He served the Father's will; and even here, you will find He is called an angel, still serving His Father's will. He will continue to serve until His Father's will is completed. Why is He called strong angel? It is because He is the strongest of all angels. He is the only One in heaven, on earth or underneath the earth who is worthy to take the book and open the seals and there is His strength. He comes down out of heaven because He has ascended and now He is ready to come down clothed with a cloud.

In Psalm 18:10-12, when the Psalmist described God as coming forth, he put it like this:

And he rode upon a cherub and did fly; yea, he flew fast upon the wings of the wind. He made darkness his secret place, his tent round about him: darkness of waters, thick clouds of the skies. From the brightness before him his thick clouds passed forth: hail and coals of fire.

We find that, when God travels, He travels with the clouds. In other words, there is brightness within the glory of the Lord, but the glory of the Lord is being shrouded with thick clouds. From the outside, you cannot see anything; it is a mystery. But of course, within the cloud, there is brightness. When God appeared on Mt. Sinai, He came with clouds; and our Lord Jesus testified to the High Priest and the Council that judged Him saying, "From henceforth ye shall see the Son of man sitting at the right hand of power, and coming on the clouds of heaven" (Matthew 26:64). Therefore, we know our Lord Jesus will come back with the cloud. Because He will come back with the cloud, there is still a certain amount of mystery there until He breaks the cloud and "like lightning" descends upon the earth. Then the mystery is completely fulfilled.

"And the rainbow upon his head." In Revelation 4, we see the throne of God in heaven, and there is a rainbow around the throne. Of course, we usually see only part of the rainbow and, at most only half of it; but there you will find a whole circle around the throne of God. Here the rainbow is upon His head like a crown upon the head of our Lord Jesus. Even in judgment there is the remembrance of mercy because rainbow speaks of mercy. You remember after God punished this earth with water, when the waters subsided, then He made a covenant with Noah and his children. God put a rainbow in the sky to alleviate the fear, to show that God is a God of mercy. So even though this strong angel comes to execute God's judgment upon this earth, yet in judgment He remembers mercy.

"And his countenance as the sun." We see, in the first chapter, the Lord Jesus is as One like the Son of man with his countenance as the sun shining in its power. Here again, His countenance is as the sun. In other words, His inward beauty is fully manifested in His life.

"And his feet as pillars of fire." Again, the first vision shows his feet as burning brass in a furnace. Here, his feet are as pillars of fire. Now brothers and sisters, when you think of pillars of fire, what picture comes back to you? Naturally, it is Exodus. There you will find God led the children of Israel out of Egypt through the wilderness with a pillar of fire and of cloud. Now to the children of Israel the pillar of fire is guidance, protection of the Lord; it is a blessing. But to the Egyptians, the pillar of fire is judgment and condemnation. So to His own, feet like pillars of fire is blessing, protection and guidance; but to His enemies, it speaks of judgment and condemnation.

"And having in his hand a little opened book." In chapter 5, when the Lamb steps forward to receive the book from God on the throne, it is a book sealed. In other words, it is a roll. It is a scroll rolled together and sealed so you do not know how big or small it is; but after the seals are all opened, then the book is an opened book and it is a small book, a little opened book. Of course, we know this book speaks of the title deed of this earth. It is the title deed of this earth. God has that in His hand and the angel, our Lord as the strong angel, comes to execute the will of God, to claim the earth as His inheritance. Now to us it is a tremendous book, but so far as God is concerned, it is a little book because our God is so much greater that even this is just a little opened book.

"And he cried with a loud voice as a lion roars." Of course, in chapter 5, we find that our Lord Jesus is like a lamb, yet one of the elders said, "Behold, the Lion of the tribe of Judah." Here you will find he roars as a lion. It speaks of His strength. It is by His strength, by His victory on Calvary's cross that He executes the will of God upon this earth to bring all things back to the original design of God. Thank God, our Lord Jesus is doing that. We know that this is what He has begun to do after His ascension and we know that it is what He is still doing today until He will bring all things to God to the glory of His Father.

"And when the seven thunders uttered their own voices." Now evidently John understood what the seven thunders said because otherwise he would not be able to write them down. He was going to do that but was not allowed to record them. It was something kept in secret. You know the same thing happened to Paul. He was caught up to the third heaven, then to paradise and heard things people should not know. He was not allowed to tell us what he heard in paradise; so dear brothers and sisters, today there are still things that we do not know. Today there are still things that God may reveal to some but will not allow to be known by all. We are still living in the time of mystery. There are still things that are being concealed, hidden. But thank God, whatever has been made known is for us. It is for us to listen and to obey.

"And he set his right foot on the sea and the left on the earth." Whenever you put your foot down, it means you take possession of it. When the children of Israel entered the Promised Land, wherever the sole of their foot stepped, it was theirs. Here you will find this strong angel, as He put His right foot on the sea and His left foot on the earth, comes to take possession of His possessions. In Psalm 2 the Father said, "Ask of me, and I will give thee nations for an inheritance, and for thy possession the ends of the earth." This happened at the ascension of our Lord Jesus; but now you will find it is describing the descension of our Lord Jesus as He puts His foot on the land and sea to take full possession of this universe.

And he lifted up his right hand to the heaven, and swore by him that lives to the ages of ages, who created the heaven and the things that are in it, and the earth and the things that are in it, and the sea and the things that are in it, that there should be no longer delay; but in the days of the voice of the seventh angel, when he is about to sound the trumpet, the mystery of God also shall be completed, as he has made known the glad tidings to his own bondmen the prophets. (Revelation 10:5-7)

In this vision, you will find the strong angel taking possession of this earth and then He proclaims, "There should be no longer delay."

You know, dear brothers and sisters, the cry of the ages is: "HOW LONG"! Since our Lord Jesus has ascended up to heaven, His church has been waiting on earth for twenty centuries, and in every century, it is the cry of the saints: "How Long, How Long!" Especially when the goings are difficult, especially when the times are very hard, especially when there are persecutions, you will find the cry of God's people on this earth is always, "How long, How long"! It appears as if He has delayed His return, but we know He does not want to postpone His return. Is there any bridegroom who is not anxious to receive his bride? Certainly, so far as our Lord Jesus is concerned, He is ever ready and most anxious to return and claim His body as His bride, but for twenty centuries He has not come. It seems as if everything is being postponed and being delayed. Why? There are two reasons.

So far as the world is concerned, it is because of the longsuffering of God. In 2 Peter 3:3-4, it says:

Knowing this first, that there shall come at the close of the days mockers with mocking, walking according to their own lusts, and saying, Where is the promise of his coming? For from the time the fathers fell asleep all things remain thus from the beginning of the creation.

There are mockers. People are mocking! They say: "Where is the promise of His coming? He is not coming back. The world is today as it was yesterday. It is the same and we will live like this today and continue on endlessly." Yet in verse 8, it says:

But let not this one thing be hidden from you, beloved, that one day with the Lord is as a thousand years, and a thousand years as one day. The Lord does not delay his promise.

Outwardly, it would appear as if the Lord has delayed His promise, but the Word of God says: "The Lord does not delay his promise, as some account of delay, but is longsuffering towards you, not willing that any should perish but that all should come to repentance." One reason why it appears to be delayed is because of the longsuffering of God. God does not want any to perish but wants all to repent. It is the patience, the longsuffering of God, and yet how the world misunderstands. They mock, they laugh, even ridicule the Lord, and yet He is still patiently waiting, waiting for repentance.

Another reason is that He is anxiously and patiently waiting for His body to be completed. He cannot come back if His bride is not yet ready. If the body is not fully matured, if the body is not fully grown unto the stature of the fulness of Christ, then He has no way to claim this body as His bride. In other words, He does not delay; we delay Him. How important it is for us to see this. Oftentimes, we think we are crying out, "How long, how long," and yet the Lord in heaven is saying, "How long, how long." We think the responsibility rests in Him, that He should have come back long ago, not knowing that the responsibility is with us. He is patiently giving us time. Oh, dear brothers and sisters, if the Lord should return today, if there is no more time, what will happen? No more time for us to be matured; for us to be obedient; for us to be grown up; for us to finish the work which God has committed to us. He is giving us time that we may grow, may fully grow and be matured.

Our Lord Jesus used a few parables:

There is an evil servant and he says in his heart, "The master delays his return." The evil servant does not deny that the master will return as he says, but the evil servant says in his heart, "The master certainly will not come soon. He will be delayed." Because of this, he begins to drink and beat his fellow servants. He begins to be careless and, at a time he does not expect, his master returns. That is the evil servant.

The good servant is ever ready. A good servant will be faithful in all the things the Lord has assigned him to do. Why? Because he will be watching and waiting and because he is watching and waiting, then in whatever hour his master should come back, the servant is ready for him. He is a good servant. "Well done, come into the joy of the Lord."

Dear brothers and sisters, may the Lord examine our hearts to see whether there is evil or good, to see whether there is in our heart the thought, "Well, the Lord will not come yet; I do not expect Him to come." Sometimes, there is such a paradox. On the one hand we pray "Thy kingdom come" as if we mean it. Yet secretly in our hearts, we are saying: "Oh, Lord, don't come now. I am not ready yet." That is the heart of an evil servant. We need to be watchful and ready at every moment.

What good news it is dear brothers and sisters, when the strong angel, "swore by him who made the heaven and the earth and said there shall be no longer delay." There will be no longer delay. He is coming. He is arriving and it is good news. Oh, brothers and sisters, just a little while and He that has promised to come will come, but He said, "May the just live by faith." THERE SHOULD BE NO LONGER DELAY. That is the good news.

But in the days of the voice of the seventh angel, when he is about to sound the trumpet, the mystery of God also shall be completed. (Revelation 10:7)

All the seven seals have been opened. The six trumpets have been blown. It remains just for the sounding of the last trumpet and then the mystery of God shall be completed. Now what is the mystery of God? "The mystery of God as he has made known the glad tidings to his own bondmen, the prophets." In other words, the mystery of God is being revealed in the glad tidings. The gospel of Jesus Christ, the glad tidings that we receive, reveals the mystery of God and the mystery of God shall be completed at the sounding of the seventh trumpet.

And the seventh angel sounded his trumpet: and there were great voices in the heaven, saying, The kingdom of the world of our Lord and of his Christ is come, and he shall reign to the ages of ages, And the twenty-four elders, who sit on their thrones before God, fell upon their faces, and worshipped God, saying, We give thee thanks, Lord God Almighty, He who is, and who was, that thou hast taken thy great power and hast reigned. And the nations have been full of wrath, and thy wrath is come, and the time of the dead to be judged, and to give the recompense to thy servants the prophets, and to the saints, and to those who fear thy name, small and great; and to destroy those that destroy the earth. (Revelation 11: 15-18)

At the sounding of the seventh trumpet, the mystery shall be completed. The mystery of God is described in chapter 11 by several things.

First: "The kingdom of the world of our Lord and of his Christ is come." This is the first thing in the mystery of God that shall be completed. This world today is under the usurper. Satan is temporarily called the ruler, the Prince of this world. The kingdoms on this earth join together and plot against God and His anointed. If you read Psalm 2, you will find how the nations, how the kings of the earth, how the princes of the kingdoms of this earth join together to plot against God and His anointed, Christ, and this is what the world is. But thank God, one day there shall no longer be delay. It is coming soon: The kingdoms of this world shall become the kingdom of our God and of His Christ. His kingdom shall come. He shall reign upon this earth. His power and authority shall be manifested.

Oh dear brothers and sisters, how often we feel, "Why doesn't God manifest His authority and power today?" Yes, He does, but not in fulness. How we hope God will stretch out His arm and show forth His strength, authority and power over all things upon this earth in fulness. That will come. When the kingdom shall become His, then His authority and power shall be fully manifested. Today, even though there are manifestations of His authority and power as evidence that all power in heaven and earth belongs to Him, yet evil still seems to rule over this earth. We still see the kingdoms of this world as being in a conspiracy against God. Again we find the great patience of God, the longsuffering of God; but the day is coming when His kingdom shall come upon this earth and its power and authority shall be fully manifested. What a day it will be! We look forward to that day.

Second: "And the nations have been full of wrath, and thy wrath is come." The nations have been full of wrath. The nations are angry. They are angry against God and the anointed of God, but their wrath has no cause. They have no reason to be angry, yet they are. The day is coming when the wrath of God is come. Today, spiritually speaking, the wrath of God is already upon all who do not believe. You remember John 3:36:

He that believes on the Son has life eternal, and he that is not subject to the Son shall not see life, but the wrath of God abides upon him.

Spiritually speaking, the wrath of God is upon all who do not believe; but the wrath of God has not been executed. Why? Because God desires that all should repent. But the day is coming when the wrath of God shall be executed, and when the wrath of God is come, who can stand? That is also the mystery of God. It is a mystery today, why there is the wrath of God and yet it is not executed. Why God allows the wrath of the nations is a mystery, but the mystery will be over, no longer delayed. The wrath of God shall come.

Third: "And the time of the dead to be judged." This, of course, looks forward even beyond the millennium. Why? Because the judgment of the dead does not come until after the millennium. In Revelation 20, there will be the great white throne. All the dead shall be given up and shall be resurrected and stand before the great white throne. All will be judged according to the books. But at the sounding of the seventh trumpet, this mystery is opening up to us, so it looks forward even beyond the millennium. Why? Because a thousand years is as a day to the Lord; therefore, one day, and the day is coming, all the dead shall be judged.

Fourth: "And to give the recompense to thy servants the prophets, and to the saints, and to those who fear thy name, small and great." It is not only judgment to the dead but it is also reward, reward to the prophets, to the saints and to all who fear the name of the Lord. Remember, dear brothers and sisters, it is more than just the gift of eternal life. How we thank God for the gift of eternal life. Eternal life is the gift of God. It is not something that we earn. It is not something that we get by our merits. We have none. It is not something as wages for the work we have done. Eternal life is the free gift of God. Dear brothers and sisters, there is more, there is more.

He will not only give us the gift of eternal life, but having received the gift of eternal life, that life in us has such a potential that it will work out unto reward. Without the eternal life in us, we cannot do the will of God; we cannot please God. However, with the eternal life of God given to us, we have the ability, the potentiality in us. With that, there is the possibility in us to do the will of God, to keep His commandments, to obey Him, to do His work; and when we are faithful, He says He will reward us. He will reward us; He will recompense us. There will be reward.

What is the reward? The reward is the glory of reigning with Christ for one thousand years. Those who are faithful to the Lord shall reign with Christ. Those who suffer with Him today shall rule and reign with Him in the kingdom age. They shall receive the crown of life, the crown of righteousness. They shall sit on thrones. They shall receive five cities, ten cities, reward! Think of that! You know, sometimes people get confused with this matter of gift and reward. People may think, "Well, do you earn your salvation?" No. Eternal life is the free gift of

God, but the glory in the kingdom is something only rewarded to those who are faithful. You may think it is your work. You may think it is you who earned the reward, but no, it is that eternal life in you. It is still the gift of God. It is still the grace of God, but you allow the grace of God to complete its work in you instead of wasting it. So, dear brothers and sisters, in the final analysis, it is still grace. Even though it is reward, which means you deserve it, it is not because of what you are, but because of what He is in you. Oh, how we look forward to that day!

Fifth: "And to destroy those that destroy the earth." How Satan has destroyed this earth. How the antichrist, how the false prophet, how the evil have destroyed the earth; but the day is coming when there shall be no longer delay. He will destroy the destroyer of the earth. At that time, you will find all things shall be restored to God's original purpose because all things were created according to His will and for His pleasure. The day is coming when all things shall be fully restored. It is through our Lord Jesus that He will reconcile all things back to the fulness of God.

Here is the honor of the church because the church shares in this work of restoring all things. God has made Christ Head "over all things to the church which is His body, the fulness of Him who fills all and in all." Therefore, the church today is to carry out what the Lord has accomplished in our own lives, in our lives together, in all things that have any relationship to us. We are to bring all things to the feet of our Lord Jesus. This is the way. This is the process. Christ is doing the work by restoring all things back to the Father and the word here is, "there shall be no longer delay, no longer delay." Dear brothers and sisters, this is a great encouragement to us, no longer delay.

HE IS COMING SOON!

He is the strong angel. He will not fail. Even though it seems outwardly that the world is getting worse and worse, further and further away from God, yet dear brothers and sisters, we know it is the Lord as the strong angel who is reclaiming all things, who is restoring all things to God; and He cannot fail. He will perfect it; and at the same time, how we need to really seize the time. This is the time, the opportunity we have to seize upon that we may grow and be fully matured that we may do the will of God and please Him because there shall be no longer delay. Dear brothers and sisters, again, if He says there shall be no longer delay, then there shall be no longer delay. Let us be watchful and let us be ready.

Our Heavenly Father, how we praise and thank Thee for showing us that Thy Son, our Lord Jesus, is the One who is restoring all things to Thy original design. Oh, how we praise and thank Thee knowing that this work is in His hand. We know that it shall be done and we do praise and thank Thee that Thou dost draw us unto Thyself to join with Thee in this work of restoring all things. Oh, Lord, we pray that all things may be first restored in us and then through us unto the praise of Thy glory. We just ask Thee to show us Thy mercy, Thy longsuffering, Thy patience with us and we do pray that by Thy grace we may be faithful. In the name of our Lord Jesus. Amen.

VISION OF THE LAMB ON MT. ZION

Revelation 14:1-5 And I saw, and behold, the Lamb standing upon mount Zion, and with him a hundred and forty-four thousand, having his name and the name of his Father written upon their foreheads. And I heard a voice out of the heaven as a voice of many waters, and as a voice of great thunder. And the voice which I heard was as of harp-singers harping with their harps; and they sing a new song before the throne, and before the four living creatures and the elders. And no one could learn that song save the hundred and forty-four thousand who were bought from the earth. These are they who have not been defiled with women, for they are virgins: these are they who follow the Lamb wheresoever it goes. These have been bought from men as firstfruits to God and to the Lamb: and in their mouths was no lie found; for they are blameless.

Revelation 14:14-16 And I saw, and behold, a white cloud, and on the cloud one sitting like the Son of man, having upon his head a golden crown, and in his hand a sharp sickle. And another angel came out of the temple, crying with a loud voice to him that sat on the cloud, Send thy sickle and reap; for the hour of reaping is come, for the harvest of the earth is dried. And he that sat on the cloud put his sickle on the earth, and the earth was reaped.

We have been emphasizing one point, and that is, how important it is that we have vision because without vision, the people perish. Especially when we are living in the last of the last days do we need to have a new and fresh and living vision of our Lord Jesus, a vision of our Lord Jesus in relation to our time, a vision of our Lord Jesus concerning the end of this age. This, we believe, is given to us in the last book of the Bible, the book of Revelation. In the book of Revelation, we find a series of visions concerning our Lord Jesus in relation to the last days.

Now we come to the fourth vision and this is found in chapter 14. Again, we find this vision has returned to the relationship of the Lord with His church, and this vision is given in two parts. In the first part, we find the Lamb standing on

Mt. Zion with 144,000; and the second part, we see One like the Son of man sitting on the cloud, casting a sharp sickle on the earth to reap the harvest. Dear brothers and sisters, we must remember that the Mt. Zion here is not the Mt. Zion on earth. There is a Mt. Zion on earth where David's throne is set, but this is the Mt. Zion in heaven, as we find in Hebrews 12:22: "But ye have come to Mount Zion; and to the city of the living God, heavenly Jerusalem." It is there that the throne of God is set.

In Psalm 2:6, we find: "And I have anointed my king upon Zion, the hill of my holiness." God has had Christ as King on Mt. Zion and we know this refers to the time He ascended up on high and there was anointed both King and Priest. Mt. Zion there is in heaven, and there we find our Lord Jesus on the throne. He is in authority. He is in power. He is in dominion. The way to Mt. Zion is by the way of the cross. Why? Because we see the Lamb there. He was oppressed; He was afflicted. He never opened His mouth. He was led as a lamb to the slaughter and as a sheep dumb in the hands of the shearers. There, through the sufferings of the cross, our Lord Jesus has arrived at Mt. Zion in heaven.

Here we find our Lord Jesus on Mt. Zion, not alone. In chapter 5, when He ascended up to heaven, we find Him as the Lamb standing, newly slain and there He received from the Father the book; but He was alone there. In chapter 14, we find He is on Mt. Zion, not alone, but with the 144,000. You know, dear brothers and sisters, there is no need for our Lord Jesus to prove that He is the victor because He already is. However, He proves that He is the victor on Calvary's cross for us, not for Himself. It is because of His victory on Calvary's cross that He is able to bring many sons into glory. Glory belongs to Him. It is always His. It is for our sake that He had to die; He had to be resurrected; He had to win that victory over Satan, over the world, over flesh, over sin, over everything. Because of what He has done on Calvary's cross, He is now able to lead us, His many sons, into glory. We find it is said in Hebrews 2:10:

For it became him, for whom are all things, and by whom are all things, in bringing many sons to glory, to make perfect the leader of their salvation through sufferings.

So in chapter 14, we find a Lamb standing on Mt. Zion with 144,000. In other words, He has led many sons to the throne.

Who are the 144,000? Of course, we know in Revelation 7, we find the number 144,000, but that number is different from the number in chapter 14. In chapter 7, we find the 144,000 refers to the children of Israel. We have the names of the tribes of Israel mentioned and they have the seal of the living God upon their heads. They are the remnant of the Jews whom God will keep through the great tribulation, the time of Jacob's trouble, but here the 144,000 is different. We will now see, in a seven-fold description, who these people really are.

First: "And with him a hundred and forty-four thousand, having his name and the name of his Father written upon their foreheads." On the foreheads of the 144,000 there is the name of the Lamb and the name of the Father, not only the name of the living God but the name of the Lamb and of His Father. We know that when you put a name upon anything, it shows that the thing belongs to that name. So a name put means "belonging." You will find the 144,000 belong to the Lamb and to His Father. He has bought us with a price, even with His precious blood, so now we belong to Him and to His Father. When you put a name upon the forehead, everybody can see it. In other words, these people belong to the Lamb and to the Father and they openly and publicly confess they are the Lamb's and the Father's. You remember our Lord Jesus said, "If you confess Me before the world, I will confess you before the Father and before the angels" (Revelation 3:5 and Matthew 10:32). These are people who not only belong to the Lord, but a people who publicly confess the name of the Lord and of the Father. They are not ashamed to confess that they belong to the Lamb and to the Father.

Second: "And the voice which I heard was as of harp-singers harping with their harps; and they sing a new song before the throne, and before the four living creatures and the elders: And no one could learn that song save the hundred and forty-four thousand who were bought from the earth." They are harp-singers. In other words, they are not only playing with their hands but they are singing with their mouths a new song. A harp is a kind of musical instrument. We call it the instrument of the heart. Why? Because as your fingers touch the strings of the harp, it is as though you are touching the strings of your heart. It is a heart instrument. In other words, they play the music from their very heart. It is out of the fulness of their very heart that music comes forth and they sing a new song, a song that nobody knows except these people. Even though you want to learn it, you won't be able to unless you learn it in the way they have. On the earth, you have music and you can learn it if you are talented. Certainly, you can learn it; but here is a song that nobody can learn. It is not a matter of musical talent. It is not a matter of good ears. It is a matter of what you have gone through. If you have never gone through what these people have, if you have never experienced the Lord in the way they have, you will not be able to sing that song even if you want to. They learn it in their lives. They learn it with the experiences of the Lord.

In a way, that is how we have the book of Psalms. Psalms in the Bible are different from the music in this world. Why? Because Psalms are different because they are the expressions of those who have experienced God in all circumstances. Out of these circumstances, they know God in a way that nobody knows and out of such experience, they pour forth in music in the Psalms. Here is a new song that only the 144,000 can sing. You remember they play the harp and sing the songs before the throne, before the four living creatures and before the twenty-four elders. In other words, they sing and they play before God. What a privilege it is. Here is an orchestra and a choir who sing and play before God. They sing unto God.

When the President of the United States entertains people, he may ask the Marines to come play or he may ask some famous singer to come and sing. What a privilege it is to come and play before the President, the honored guests and the people of high position. Dear brothers and sisters, we may not be called to the White House to sing and play, but we are called to sing and play before the throne and what a privilege that is: to sing and play before the throne, before the four living creatures and the twenty-four elders. The living creatures represent the whole creation; the twenty-four elders represent the rulers of the universe. In other words, here you will find we are playing and singing, with the universe listening to us, and God is pleased with what we sing and play. What is this new song? It must be a song that is praising, telling and proclaiming of the love, mercy, grace, longsuffering and faithfulness of God and our Lord Jesus. It is an endless new song. It will never grow old.

Third: "These are they who have not been defiled with women, for they are virgins." Now you cannot explain this in literal terms because it is too spiritual. Why is that? In other words, here are a people who have not been defiled. They are the five wise virgins who you will find in Matthew 25. You remember Paul told the Corinthian believers:

For I am jealous as to you with a jealousy which is of God; for I have espoused you unto one man, to present you a chaste virgin to Christ. But I fear lest by any means, as the serpent deceived Eve by his craft, so your thoughts should be corrupted from simplicity as to the Christ. (2 Corinthians 11:3-4)

But here, dear brothers and sisters, you will find the 144,000 remain as chaste virgins to the One to whom they have been betrothed. They are chaste, pure, single; they have not been enticed from the simplicity that is of Christ. Their heart is wholly set upon the Lord and, because of that, they are privileged to stand with the Lamb on Mt. Zion.

Fourth: "These are they who follow the Lamb wheresoever it goes." Wherever the Lamb goes, these people go. When the Lamb was on earth going through Gethsemane, going through Calvary, going through the tomb, these people were following the Lamb. They follow the Lamb to Calvary; they follow the Lamb even to death. It is not a matter of your choosing where you go, if it suits you, you follow Him; if it doesn't suit you, you go your own way. Not so! These people, while on earth, follow the Lamb wheresoever it goes. Dear brothers and sisters, wherever the

Lamb goes, will you go with Him? Will you go with Him if it means affliction; if it means suffering; if it means tribulation, if it means persecutions; if it means death; if it means tribulation; if it means loss of self; it means shame, disgrace, reproach?

Are you willing to follow the Lamb wherever it goes? It is true, sometimes the Lamb seems to go to a place of still waters, of green pastures, but sometimes the Lamb will go through the valley of the shadow of death. If we follow Him to the cross, we will follow Him to the throne as we see here in the 144,000. They follow Him wherever He goes.

Fifth: "These have been bought from men as firstfruits to God and to the Lamb." Who are these people? They are the firstfruits. In agriculture, suppose you have a field of wheat. As the time of harvest draws near, you will find a patch of wheat that ripens first, and these are the firstfruits. It is cut first, and according to the law of Moses, when the firstfruits were ripened and cut, it was brought to the temple and offered to God before anyone could eat of it. In other words, the firstfruits are always the best of the crop and these are meant for God and the Lamb. Here you will find of all the believers whom the Lord has bought with His precious blood, there will be the firstfruits of the believers and they are those that are first ripened. The firstfruits are always the best and they are for God and the Lamb. They are presented to God and the Lamb and that is why they are on Mt. Zion. They are there.

You know the wheat, after the sun has scorched it, is dry. It is so dry and the root is so loosened from the earth that when you pull it, it will come up. The 144,000 are ripened before the rest of the field. Why? Probably, they suffered more than the rest for the Lord's sake. The rest may try to evade the cross, but these followed the Lamb to the cross and, because of that, they are dried first. They are ready; therefore, they are raptured. They are raptured and taken to Mt. Zion. Brothers and sisters, in Revelation 12, you will find the man child. When the man child is born, he is taken to the throne and this is the 144,000 here. They are there on Mt. Zion.

Sixth: "And in their mouths was no lie found." Why is it that this point seems to be labored here, in their mouths was no lie found? Why is it so important to be mentioned here? The reason is the word of their testimony. In chapter 12, it says:

They overcame Satan because of the blood of the Lamb and because of the word of their testimony and they loved not their lives even unto death. (v.11)

THE WORD OF THEIR TESTIMONY! These people have a testimony to give and they utter their testimony. What is the word of their testimony? It is:

Jesus is the first and the last, and the living one. He is the One who became dead and is now living to the ages of the ages and has the keys of death and of hades. JESUS IS LORD!

Whenever Satan is active, these people utter the word of their testimony and Satan is defeated. Because of this, how important their mouth is. If there is a lie in their mouth, then the word of their testimony will not be able to overcome. They speak the truth. What they say is true, not only objectively true but subjectively true. In other words, brothers and sisters, you may say something that is true, but if you have no experience of it, it is not so true. When you say something that you experience, it is truly true, really true and if it is really true, there is affect; there is impact. I believe that is the meaning of "There is no lie in their mouths." They are not saying something which is just correct. Whatever they say, they have experienced and, therefore, there is power behind it. How important it is that we have the word of our testimony.

Seventh: "For they are blameless." Ephesians 1:4 states, "God has chosen us in him before the world's foundation, that we should be holy and blameless before him in love." Also, in Ephesians 5:26-27, it says, "Christ will sanctify His church by the water of His Word that He might present to Himself a glorious church without spot or wrinkle, or any such things; that it might be holy and blameless." In other words, it is the purpose of God that we should be blameless before Him. There is nothing to be blamed. How can we be blameless before Him if it is not because of the blood of the Lamb. Oh, how He has cleansed us. He has cleansed us in such a way that we are now without blame. God cannot blame us anymore. Another thing, it is in love. Because of His love, how He forgives us. He has a way to bring us to that place of being holy and blameless before Him. These are the seven-fold descriptions of the 144,000.

So who are these? They represent the overcomers of the church. One hundred and forty-four thousand is the multiple of twelve, and twelve is a perfect number. In other words, the 144,000 represent the overcomers of the church through the ages. If you want to take the 144,000 literally, then you may say they represent the cream; therefore, they represent the whole of the overcomers. But I don't believe you can take it literally since this is taken in a way that it is a perfect number. In other words, God will have His overcomers in perfect number, in fulness, in spite of everything we see today.

When we look at ourselves, when we look at the church of God in general, sometimes we wonder where will God ever have His overcomers. Where will the number of the overcomers be fulfilled? But He knows how to get them and He is getting them. Here the 144,000 are standing with the Lamb on Mt. Zion. There they are. It is by the overcomers of the church that the King is being introduced upon the earth. How blessed it is that, by the grace of God, we may be ranked among the 144,000. In other words, that we may be among the overcomers of the church. This is just part of the vision of our Lord Jesus, the Lamb standing with the 144,000.

Next you come to the second part of that vision: "And I saw, and behold, a white cloud, and on the cloud one sitting like the Son of man." Notice the difference. In the first part, you see Mt. Zion, which is the throne; but here you see the white cloud and, on the cloud, One sitting like the Son of man. In Matthew 24:30, our Lord Jesus said, "And they shall see the Son of man coming on the clouds of heaven with power and great glory." Also, in Matthew 26:64, when He testified before the Jewish Council, He said, "From henceforth you shall see the Son of man sitting at the right hand of power, and coming on the clouds of heaven." In other words, our Lord Jesus will come with the clouds of heaven. He will ride the clouds to come upon this earth, so you can see that He has descended from Mt. Zion to the cloud.

You know, when our Lord Jesus ascended up to heaven, He ascended to heaven on Mt. Olive and, probably, about 500 brethren saw Him going up. They saw Him taken up by God. He began to ascend and, when this happened, they all looked up at Him. Now when He had ascended for a little distance, a cloud took Him. They couldn't see Him anymore. The cloud was rising up and up but they couldn't see Him because He was hidden by the cloud. Yet these men of Galilee still looked up and looked up and looked up. Two men in white appeared and said:

Men of Galilee, why do you stand looking into heaven? This Jesus who has been taken up from you into heaven, shall thus come in the manner in which you have beheld him going into heaven. (Acts 1:11)

In other words, the manner in which our Lord Jesus was taken up will be the same in which He will return. How was the Lord Jesus taken up? He was taken up from the earth, Mt. Olive, to the cloud. That is the first stage. The second stage is from the cloud to heaven to the throne. In His coming back, it will be in like manner; that is to say, He will descend from heaven to the cloud first and then the second stage will be from the cloud to the earth on Mt. Olive. The 144,000 were standing with the Lamb on Mt. Zion in heaven, so brothers and sisters, the firstfruits of the church are raptured to the throne in heaven with the Lamb.

Then after this has happened (as you remember in chapter 12 when the man child is taken up), there will be war in the air because the air is where Satan has his headquarters. Michael and his angels will fight with Satan and his followers and there will be no more place for Satan in the air. He will be cast down upon the earth. In other words, the air will be cleared. Why is it cleared? It is cleared so that the Lord may descend to the cloud, with the clouds of heaven, to the air. Here you will find our Lord

Jesus is already descending to the cloud, but He is still sitting on the cloud. In other words, the cloud has not been broken up yet; therefore, on earth you cannot see Him. One day, He will break the cloud and will be like lightning everybody will see and He will descend upon this earth.

Now why did He come to the cloud? Here you will find He was like the Son of man. Of course, we see that in chapter 1. That is the Lord. There is no doubt about that, but He has a golden crown upon His head here. You know, there is something very interesting:

And in the midst of the seven lamps one like the Son of man............his head and hair white like white wool, as snow. (Revelation 1:13-14)

You can see His hair and there is no crown. Now why is that? In Hebrews 2, our Lord Jesus, after He had suffered death for everyone, was crowned with glory and honor. In other words, so far as our Lord Jesus is concerned, He is already crowned. He is crowned with glory and honor; but why is it in chapter 1 there is no crown? It is because He is standing in the midst of the seven golden lampstands and there we see

Him in relation to the church. It is in the beginning of the church and the Lord is examining, looking at His church and, if she is faithful, she will be crowned. You remember the promise to the overcomer:

Be thou faithful unto death, and I will give to thee the crown of life. (Revelation 2:10)

Notice the letter to the church in Philadelphia: "Hold fast what thou hast, that no one take thy crown." In other words, the reward is still in the future and because our Lord Jesus is with His church, therefore, you will find He is not crowned, as if He is waiting to be crowned with us. Here it is at the end of the church period because the Lord is coming to reap the harvest. In other words, the testing has already been done, who will be crowned and who will not be crowned is to be decided very shortly at the judgment seat of Christ. Therefore, our Lord Jesus comes with the crown. He is crowned and He is going to crown those who are faithful to Him.

Now He has in His hand a sharp sickle. In other words, He comes to reap, to reap the harvest. It is to reap the wheat.

Another angel came out of the temple, crying with a loud voice to him who sits on the cloud, Send in thy sickle and reap for the hour of reaping is come for the harvest of the earth is dried. (Revelation 14:15)

Even here, He is waiting for an order from the Father. You remember our Lord Jesus said no one, not angels, not men, not even the Son, but the Father knew the hour and the day of His coming. His time is in God's hand. He is waiting for an order from the Father and, when the order comes, then He casts the sickle and reaps the harvest. God has a timetable, but it is not mechanical; that is to say, you do not set a year, a day, an hour and say, "The Lord will come January 1, 2000." No. God has a timetable, but it is spiritual. In other words, when the condition is fulfilled, then the time has come, the time of harvest is come. Why? It is because the harvest is dried. Do you see? This is God's timetable and, because of that, dear brothers and sisters, there is such a responsibility upon us. Why is it that God's time has still not come? How often we say, "How long will you delay your coming?" The cry of the church throughout the ages is: "How long? Why is it so long?" Brothers and sisters, it is because God's timetable is living. It is based on conditions. It is because the church is not yet ready, therefore, He cannot come to reap it.

You cannot reap a field when the harvest is not dry. You have to wait, like a farmer waits patiently, for the time to reap. Oh, how patiently he will wait. Sometimes he gets anxious but he cannot do anything. He has to wait; but when the harvest is ready, how he will rejoice in it. Dear brothers and sisters, God is waiting, waiting for us to be dried. Oh, we are too wet. We are too wet with the cares of this life; the anxieties of this life; the riches of this world; all the other things that dilute us.

We are not dry enough to be cut, but when we are dried, then the time is come and the Lord will cast His sickle and reap the harvest. Of course, when He harvests them, He will take them to the cloud in the sky to the air. This is 1 Thessalonians 4:16-17:

For the Lord himself, with an assembling shout, with archangel's voice and with trump of God, shall descend from heaven; and the dead in Christ shall rise first; then we, the living who remain, shall be caught up together with them in the clouds, to meet the Lord in the air.

Brothers and sisters, in this vision of our Lord Jesus, we find His relationship with the overcomers of the church and His relationship with the rest of His church. The point is: Do you know the Lord as the Lamb on Mt. Zion, or do you only know Him as the Son of man sitting on the cloud? Will you be with the Lord on Mt. Zion or will you be with the Son of man in the air? It makes a great difference!

That is the difference between the firstfruits and the harvest and we need to look to the Lord that, by His grace (it is grace), we will allow this grace to have a free hand in our lives. Grace can bring us to the first rank to be overcomers and to stand with the Lamb on Mt. Zion.

Dear brothers and sisters, do not linger and linger with the things of this world until you have to pass through the great tribulation. Thank God for the great tribulation. Why? It is because the great tribulation is like the sun which scorches the rest to dry. If you are not willing to suffer with Him today, you may have to remain for the great tribulation to dry you. Thank God, it is still for a positive purpose.

We must be dried! We must be dried! But why not today? May the Lord have mercy on us!

Our Heavenly Father, we do praise and thank Thee for showing us Thy relationship with us in the last days. Oh, how Thou dost long that we may be the firstfruits, that we may be dried first, that we may be presented to Thee, even to Thy temple for Thy purpose, for Thy satisfaction and joy. Oh, Lord, we pray that by grace we may be ranked among those. Do not allow us to love the world, to love ourselves and to miss the opportunity; trying to escape troubles and tribulations, trying to live for ourselves, going our own way and, Lord, we remain behind and be scorched by the sun of the great tribulation. Oh, Lord, give us wisdom that we may have a wise heart, that we may follow Thee today; wheresoever You go, we go; where You are, we are; where You stay, we stay. We ask in Thy precious Name. Amen.

VISION OF THE LAST WAR

Revelation 19:11-21 And I saw the heaven opened, and behold, a white horse, and one sitting on it, called Faithful and True, and he judges and makes war in righteousness. And his eyes are a flame of fire, and upon his head many diadems, having a name written which no one knows but himself; and he is clothed with a garment dipped in blood; and his name is called The Word of God; and the armies which are in the heaven followed him upon white horses, clad in white, pure, fine linen. And out of his mouth goes a sharp two-edged sword, that with it he might smite the nations; and he shall shepherd them with an iron rod; and he treads the winepress of the fury of the wrath of God the Almighty. And he has upon his garment, and upon his thigh, a name written, King of kings, and Lord of lords. And I saw an angel standing in the sun; and he cried with a loud voice, saying to all the birds that fly in mid-heaven, Come, gather yourselves to the great supper of God, that ye may eat flesh of kings, and flesh of chiliarchs, and flesh of strong men, and flesh of horses and of those that sit upon them, and flesh of all, both free and bond, and small and great. And I saw the beast and the kings of the earth and their armies gathered together to make war against him that sat upon the horse, and against his army. And the beast was taken, and the false prophet that was with him, who wrought the signs before him by which he deceived them that received the mark of the beast, and those that worship his image. Alive were both cast into the lake of fire which burns with brimstone; and the rest were slain with the sword of him that sat upon the horse, which goes out of his mouth; and all the birds were filled with their flesh.

Revelation 20:1-3 And I saw an angel descending from the heaven, having the key of the abyss, and a great chain in his hand. And he laid hold of the dragon, the ancient serpent who is the devil and Satan, and bound him a thousand years, and cast him into the abyss, and shut it and sealed it over him, that he should not any more deceive the nations until the thousand years were completed; after these things he must be loosed for a little time.

Shall we pray:

Lord, how we praise and thank Thee that we are so privileged to gather around Thyself to remember Thee and worship Thee. Oh, how we praise and thank Thee for the privilege that through Thy word we may see Thee afresh. We do ask that at this moment the anointing of the Lord be upon us that we may truly see Thee as we together consider Thy word. We want Thee to be exalted. We want Thee to fill our hearts. We want Thee to draw us out of ourselves and into Thyself. In the Name of our Lord Jesus. Amen.

The last book of the Bible is the Revelation. It is the revelation of Jesus Christ which God gave to Him to show to us. In this book, we are to see the Lord Jesus. We are to see Him in relation to our day. Being the last book of the Bible, it deals with the end times and we are living in the end times. It is imperative that we see our Lord Jesus in relation to our times, in relation to the days in which we are living. As we see what kind of Lord He is to us, I believe it will strengthen our faith, encourage us with hope and increase our love to Him.

Previously, we have covered four visions of our Lord Jesus as revealed in this book of Revelation. In the fifth vision of our Lord Jesus, John said, "I saw the heaven opened." Now in this book, we find this is not the first time it is said the heavens were opened, but we know there is a difference here. So far as the Scripture is concerned, we find there are at least three heavens. Of course, we hear people talk about seven heavens, or even more, but that is not scriptural.

THIRD HEAVEN - Where the throne of God is.

SECOND HEAVEN - Where the celestial stars are.

FIRST HEAVEN - The air above us where the clouds are.

The heaven here that John saw opened is not the third heaven. Why? It is because, in chapter 4, he said the heaven opened. John was taken up into the heaven and saw the throne and the One who sits upon the throne. In other words, in chapter 4, it is the third heaven.

When John saw the heaven opened here and said, "Behold a white horse," this is the first heaven. Why? As we read the book of Revelation, in chapter 14, about the 144,000 standing with the Lamb on Mt. Zion, we find we find that this is not the Mt. Zion on earth. It is the Mt. Zion in heaven. But after that scene, we see "the Son of man sitting on the cloud." In other words, first, we find Him in the third heaven upon the throne, but then He descends from the throne to the cloud. That is the first stage of His return. We find in 1 Thessalonians that while He is sitting on the cloud, the harvest is ready and all who are dead in Christ and those who are alive and still remain at that moment will be taken up to meet the Lord in the air. Brothers and sisters, let's remember this: The 144,000 who represent the overcomers of the church who come with the Lord from the throne to the air and those who are alive and remain on earth and the dead in Christ who are raised first will all be caught up to the air to be with the Lord. In other words, there in the air will be the great gathering of the saints. While the saints are gathered together with the Lord in the air, there will be the time which we find in Scripture, the judgment seat of Christ.

Judgment must begin with the house of God. (1 Peter 4:17)

It will be at this time, when we are all gathered together, that we shall all stand before the judgment seat of Christ. Now for the sake of some who do not know the difference, maybe I should explain a little.

We who believe in the Lord Jesus will never stand before the great white throne judgment. Why? Since Christ was judged for us on Calvary's cross, we are delivered from the judgment, the eternal judgment of the great white throne; but that does not mean that we as the children of God will not be judged. We will be judged, but in a different way. We will be judged before the judgment seat of Christ. There is a difference between seat and throne. Throne is judicial; seat is family. Therefore, as children of God, one day, we will all appear before the judgment seat of Christ. We will be judged according to what we have done on earth, whether we built with gold, silver, precious stones or wood, straw, stubble.

There we shall be judged and receive our reward or suffer loss, yet not eternally.

While the judgment seat of Christ is going on in the air, the outpouring of the wrath of God, as seen in the seven vials in the book of Revelation, will be going on on the earth. At the end of the seven vials, heaven opens; that is to say, the Lord will appear upon this earth. It is the time of the appearing of His coming, the Apocalypse. He will break the cloud and come down upon this earth, and the way in which He will come will be riding on a white horse.

Dear brothers and sisters, you know in the Scriptures, an ass signifies peace, but a horse signifies war. You remember in Zechariah 9:9:

Behold, thy King cometh to thee: he is just, and having salvation; lowly and riding upon an ass, even upon a colt the foal of an ass.

In the first coming of our Lord Jesus, He came as King and rode upon an ass. You know, that was literally fulfilled when He entered into Jerusalem for the last time. You remember how the people gathered around Him as He rode upon this colt and shouted, "Hosanna." It was at that time that He came as King to offer peace to Jerusalem and to this world. One day, when He shall come again, He shall ride upon a horse. In other words, He will come back to war against this rebellious world.

"A white horse." White in the Scripture always speaks of purity. Here, when our Lord Jesus shall return to wage war upon this world, it will be a war of righteousness. We often hear people say: "This is a war of righteousness. It is a righteous war. We fight a righteous war." However, in the scriptural sense, dear brothers and sisters, there is no war on earth that is righteous. There is so much selfishness involved in any and every war that this is not so. Thank God, one day there will be a war that is righteous, a war of righteousness when our Lord Jesus will come with His followers to fight against Satan and his followers. This is the last war, the war of Armageddon.

"And one sitting on it, called Faithful and True." We have seen this before. In Revelation 1, we saw that He is the faithful witness. In

Revelation 3:14, He says He is "the Amen, the faithful and true witness." These are the names of our Lord Jesus. These qualities are His characters. In other words, our Lord Jesus is characterized by being faithful. In what sense is He faithful? He is faithful to the Father. He is faithful to do the will of the Father. He is faithful to do all the wills of the Father. He is faithful to the Father in the sense that He does not come to do anything of His own will. "Not My will but Your will be done." That is His faithfulness and that is His character.

He is true, true in the sense that He is true to Himself. He is real to Himself. There is no pretense in Him. Everything of Him is real, is true, and even His enemies have to acknowledge that He is true. There is no falsehood in Him. He is the truth. He is the reality. These are the characters of our Lord Jesus.

"And he judges and makes war in righteousness." He judges. How does He judge? In John 5, the Lord said He did not judge by Himself. He judges according to the Father's will and, because of that, His judgment is true. What

He sees that is not according to His Father's will, He judges; therefore, His war is the war of righteousness.

"And his eyes are a flame of fire." We have seen that before. In Revelation 1 through 3 where it says, "His eyes are a flame of fire," it is in relation to His church. Brothers and sisters, so far as the church is concerned, the eyes of our Lord Jesus are as a flame of fire. In other words, He sees us thoroughly. He sees everything. There is nothing that He does not see. He has such discernment. He sees so sharply and clearly and thank God for that flame of fire. Why? Because it purifies us. Sometimes, we are afraid of these eyes. I remember reading this story somewhere:

There was one who was in prison and he said what he feared most or suffered most from while there were the eyes of the guards. Even with the door closed, there was a hole there and whenever he would look up at the door, he would see the eyes peeping through at him. He said that was the thing of which he was the most afraid.

Dear brothers and sisters, the eyes of the Lord are as flames of fire. He looks at us and sees us through, but we don't need to be afraid because His look recovers us. You remember He looked at Peter after he had denied Him the three times. The Lord just looked at him, looked into him and Peter went out and wept, but Peter was recovered. Thank God for the piercing eyes of our Lord Jesus. Here in chapter 19 where it says His eyes are as a flame of fire, it is in relation to the world. It is different. In other words, He sees what the world is so clearly. He sees through the world but it is not for recovery. It is for war. It is for judgment. It is for punishment.

"And upon his head many diadems." A diadem is a crown without a top. If you wear a crown with a top to it, you can only wear one. If you wear a diadem, you can wear many because there is no top. Every diadem represents His Kingship in a certain territory. Here we see our Lord Jesus is King over many territories and many areas. He reigns over realms and realms. He wears many diadems.

"Having a name written which no one knows but himself." Thank God there are some names of our Lord Jesus that are revealed and, because they are revealed, we know what these names are. We know His name is Jesus, who saves us from our sins. We know His name is Immanuel, God with us. We know His name is Faithful and True. Thank God for all the revelations of His name because a name represents the person. You know the person by his name, and we do thank the Lord that God has revealed many names of our Lord Jesus to us that we may know Him in many aspects. However, in spite of all that has been made known to us, there is a name that has not been revealed. There is a name of our Lord Jesus that is unknown. No one knows it but Himself. Brothers and sisters, there is always something in our Lord Jesus that we do not know. It is beyond our knowledge. We only know what is revealed, but what is hidden belongs to God.

There is always something hidden in the Godhead for the Father, Son and Holy Spirit to enjoy and it is too sacred for us to know. We should be content. You know, we should be like "weaned children leaning upon the breast of their mother, not exercising themselves in high and lofty things" (Psalm 131). Even what has been revealed to us and what is going to be revealed to us will take eternity to know, and yet, even in eternity, He is still unknown. There is a name no one knows but Himself. Oh, how I thank God that He is God. Sometimes, we think because of such mercy and grace that is showered upon us when we receive the life of Christ, we are deified. We feel as if we are God's now and there is no more of God that we do not know. But, dear brothers and sisters, we are not deified. God is God. There is always something in Him that we do not know and that something is too deep for us to probe.

"And he is clothed with a garment dipped in blood." Why is He clothed with a garment dipped in blood? If you refer to Isaiah 63:1-3, you will find there is a prophecy concerning this very event:

Who is this that cometh from Edom, with deep-red garments from Bozrah, this that is glorious in his apparel, traveling in the greatness of his strength? I that speak in righteousness, mighty to save. Wherefore is redness in thine apparel, and thy garments like him that treadeth in the winevat? I have trodden the winepress alone, and of the peoples not a man was with me; and I have trodden them in mine anger, and trampled them in my fury; and their blood is sprinkled upon my garments, and I have stained all my apparel.

In other words, you will find that His garment is dipped in blood because, when He shall come back to take revenge upon His enemies, the blood of His enemies shall be sprinkled upon His garments and stain them. That is the result of that war. Oh, brothers and sisters, once upon a time about two thousand years ago when He first came into this world to offer peace, the world rejected the Prince of Peace. The world murdered Him. His blood was shed on Calvary's cross and His body was covered with His own blood. But the day will come when He shall return and shed the blood of the enemies that rejected Him and refused to accept Him because judgment is finally come into this world.

"And his name is called The Word of God." We are familiar with that name.

In the beginning was the Word, and the Word was with God, and the Word was God. (John 1:1)

The One who sits upon the white horse is none other than the Word of God. From eternity to eternity, He is God. He is the very expression of God. He is the One who reveals and declares the Father. He is the living Word and He still is. His name is called the Word of God.

"And out of his mouth goes a sharp two-edged sword that with it he might smite the nations." When He shall return, He will war against Satan and his followers and the weapon of His war is a sharp two-edged sword proceeding out of His mouth. Now you remember 2 Thessalonians 2:8:

And then the lawless one shall be revealed, whom the Lord Jesus shall consume with the breath of his mouth, and shall annul by the appearing of his coming.

When the Lord shall return here, He shall consume the lawless one, that is the antichrist, with the breath of His mouth. Now the breath of His mouth is the sharp two-edged sword. In other words, with His breath, with His Word, He destroys His enemies. There is such power in His Word. May we say it is like an ideological war. It is a war of ideas and here you will find faithful and true have prevailed against unfaithfulness and falsehood. Throughout the ages, faithfulness and unfaithfulness, truth and falsehood are fighting against each other. Oftentimes, we think unfaithfulness, disobedience, falsehood, rebellion and lies seem to prevail but that only appears to be. In the finality, we will find that faithfulness and truth shall prevail. The Lord will use His breath, His Word like a sharp two-edged sword to cut down all His enemies.

"And he shall shepherd them with an iron rod." Now of course, this refers to the millennium. Those that are not killed by that sharp two-edged sword that comes out of His mouth, those nations that will be removed into the kingdom will be ruled with an iron rod.

"And he treads the winepress of the fury of the wrath of God the Almighty." If you will refer to Revelation 14:17, which is after the harvest, you will find the same thing:

And another angel came out of the temple which is in the heaven, he also having a sharp sickle. And another angel came out of the altar, having power over fire, and called with a loud cry to him that had the sharp sickle, saying, Send thy sharp sickle, and gather the bunches of the vine of the earth; for her grapes are fully ripened. And the angel put his sickle to the earth, and gathered the vine of the earth, and cast the bunches into the great winepress of the fury of God; and the winepress was trodden without the city, and blood went out of the winepress to the bits of the horses for a thousand six hundred stadia.

Here, our Lord Jesus in His return will tread the winepress. The grapes that are gathered represent the world. He will judge the world and the blood will come to the bits of the horses for a thousand six hundred stadia. That is the last battle, the battle of Armageddon.

"And he has upon his garment, and upon his thigh, a name written, King of kings, and Lord of lords." Here is another name, King of kings, Lord of lords. Who are these kings? Who are these lords? In any way, our Lord Jesus is supreme. Even though today He is the rejected King, one day He, who has been rejected, shall reign and rule as the King of kings and Lord of lords. All this refers to the appearing of His coming. He shall appear upon this earth; He shall destroy His enemies and rule and reign as King of kings and Lord of lords.

"And the armies which are in the heaven followed him upon white horses, clad in white, pure, fine linen." When our Lord Jesus came to earth, when the Word became flesh, He was alone. When He went to the cross, He was alone. But here you will find when He shall appear on this earth, He will come as the victor of Calvary, the conqueror. When He shall return as the conqueror of this world, He will have His army with Him. Who are these armies? They will ride upon white horses and be clad in white, pure, fine linen. You see, in His return, He is not alone. He will bring with Him His army, heavenly armies. But the army here cannot refer to the angelic host. It is true, He shall return with myriads of angels; but aside from these heavenly hosts, He will return with a heavenly army and the army is composed of men and women such as we. How do we know this? Please refer to Revelation 17:14:

These shall make war with the Lamb, and the Lamb shall overcome them; for he is Lord of lords and King of kings: and they that are with him called, and chosen, and faithful.

The army that is with Him in that triumphant battle are those who are called, chosen and faithful. We are all called saints. To be very strict, we are not called "to be saints" but we are called "saints." He has called us, called us by His love, called us by His glory. We who are the Lord's are the called. We do not volunteer to come to Him. He calls us and thank God that He has; but the thing is, many are called but few are chosen. Why? It is because those who are called do not all respond to the grace He has given to us. In other words, we are called, but we are not chosen until we yield ourselves to His love and grace and let His love and grace do its perfect work in us. Many are called but few are chosen!

And fewer are the faithful! Are we faithful to the very end? Paul said:

But when God, who set me apart even from my mother's womb, and called me by his grace. (Galatians 1:15)

And I thank Christ Jesus our Lord, who has given me power, that he has counted me faithful. (1 Timothy 1:12)

Are we the called? Are we the chosen? Are we the faithful?

Now these people are clad in white, pure, fine linen and we see that also in Revelation 19:8:

And his wife has made herself ready. And it was given to her that she should be clothed in fine linen, bright and pure; for the fine linen is the righteousness of the saints.

Practical righteousness! In other words, these are the people, they are not perfect, but they allow the Holy Spirit to work the righteousness that is of Christ into their very being.

These are the people who are cleansed by the precious blood of the Lamb, who have the word of their testimony, who loved not their lives even unto death.

In other words, the armies that come with the Lord in His appearing are the overcomers of the church. The reason they are privileged to follow the Lord in this last battle is because they have won while on earth just like the Lord won His battle while He was on earth. When our Lord Jesus was on earth, how fierce was the conflict. The battle even began when He was born. As a baby, He had to flee to Egypt, and the battle continued on throughout His life.

When He first began His ministry in Nazareth, they took Him out to the cliff to push Him down, but our Lord Jesus just walked right through them. Again and again you will see in the records of the Gospels how the enemy tried to murder Him, to cut Him off before His time. Finally, in the garden of Gethsemane, how He prayed, how He was weakened, how His blood oozed from His pores. He had to be strengthened by the angel; otherwise, He would have died in the garden of Gethsemane. On Calvary's cross, He cried out, "My God, My God, why hast Thou forsaken Me?" The battle was fierce but our Lord Jesus fought that battle alone, all by Himself. He trod the winepress alone; but before He died, He said, "It is finished." The shout of VICTORY: It is finished! The battle is won!

In Colossians 2, we see how He spoiled principalities and authorities, led them captive, displayed them as His captives and made a public show of them and triumphed by the cross. Our Lord Jesus won the battle while He was on earth! Now when He comes back in that last battle of Armageddon, how will that battle be fought? The battle has already been won, so He just speaks a word by the breath of His mouth and His enemies are destroyed. In other words, it is based on the victory of Calvary. He needs only to speak the word and the enemy is finished.

Brothers and sisters, today, while we are on earth, there is a fierce battle going on so far as our spiritual living is concerned. If you follow the Lord today, you will find you are in a battle.

It is an endless battle and it is fierce. Paul said, "I have fought the good fight." Oh, how we need to fight the good fight. How the enemy is trying to destroy us, trying to entice us, trying to trip us, trying in every way to destroy us. There is a battle going on all the time. Have we fought the good fight?

Of course, even though we are fighting that fight, the battle is the Lord's. The Lord has won the victory. We are fighting from victory to victory. It is just a matter of standing in the victory of the Lord, declaring His victory, claiming His victory, applying His victory over all the fiery darts of the enemy. If we know how to stand in the victory of Christ, how to claim His victory over the assaults of the enemy, then we fight the good fight. Our Lord Jesus had to fight alone, but with us, we are actually standing to see the victory of Christ applied. Those who have experienced such victory will be privileged to follow the Lord to that last battle, not to fight, but to witness the victory of the Lord. You will find they do not fight at all. They just follow.

In other words, dear brothers and sisters, the pattern is set today. How do we fight the good fight? You just follow the Lamb. That is all. You don't fight; you just follow. As you learn the pattern, then the day will come when our Lord will return; you will return with Him and just follow and witness His great victory over His enemies. That is the way the last battle will be fought.

What will be the result of that battle? You will see that the antichrist, the false prophet and the two beasts will be seized and cast into the lake of fire, the second death. The dragon, the serpent, Satan, will be seized and chained and put into the bottomless pit, sealed there for a thousand years. Those that follow the beast to fight against our Lord Jesus will be killed and there will be a great supper prepared for all the birds of prey. Those nations that do not follow the beast when he comes to that battle will be as the sheep nations, and when the kingdom shall be established, they will be moved into the kingdom as the nations and the Lord shall rule over them with a rod of iron. If you follow on to chapter 20, you will find thrones will be there. In other words, that will be the time when the saints shall be rewarded and they shall reign with Christ for a thousand years.

Dear brothers and sisters, this is the revelation of our Lord Jesus in relation to the appearing of His coming. Today, there is a fierce battle going on between faithfulness and unfaithfulness, truth and falsehood, obedience and rebellion, Christ and Satan, followers of the Lord and followers of the world. But thank God, in spite of the fact that these evils seem to prevail, we know the result and we know who will come out with the upper hand. Why? It is because when we look at Calvary, we know the battle has already been won. It is just a matter of time and, because of this, dear brothers and sisters, let our hearts be encouraged. As long as we live on earth, let us learn to follow the Lamb whithersoever He goes. As you follow the Lamb, you will be drawn into the fierce battle of the ages but there is no need to fear. Why? It is because He has already overcome and all you need to do is stand and see the victory of the Lord. May this be our encouragement!

Our Heavenly Father, how we praise and thank Thee. Even though at times, when we look around, we may wonder and yet, Lord, we praise and thank Thee because Thou hast told us so clearly that Thou hast already won the battle and Thou art coming to conclude everything and to bring in Thy kingdom. Oh, Lord, we do pray that during this short time that we may be kept faithful to the very end. We ask Thee, oh Lord, that Thy grace will complete and perfect this work in each and every one of us. Oh, that we may be numbered among those who are counted as the called, the chosen and the faithful. We pray that we may today experience the victory of the Lord, that one day we may witness that great victory that shall come on this earth. We give Thee all the praise and glory. In the Name of our Lord Jesus. Amen.

VISION OF THE
GREAT WHITE THRONE

Revelation 20:11-15 And I saw a great white throne, and him that sat on it, from whose face the earth and the heaven fled, and place was not found for them. And I saw the dead, great and small, standing before the throne, and books were opened; and another book was opened, which is that of life. And the dead were judged out of the things written in the books according to their works. And the sea gave up the dead which were in it, and death and hades gave up the dead which were in them; and they were judged each according to their works: and death and hades were cast into the lake of fire. This is the second death, even the lake of fire. And if anyone was not found written in the book of life, he was cast into the lake of fire.

Now let us look at the sixth vision of the Lord Jesus in the book of Revelation. In the fifth vision, we see Him as One who rides upon a white horse—One who comes with His army to that last battle before the millennium, the battle of Armageddon. We find how╞by the sword that comes out of His mouth, even with His breath╞ He destroys His enemies and sets up His kingdom upon this earth. The Lord Jesus taught His church to pray, "Thy kingdom come." As we have already seen, after that last battle, His kingdom has finally been manifested upon this earth. It is as we see in the book of Isaiah:

Righteousness shall rule over this earth and the knowledge of God shall fill the earth as waters fill the sea.

It is the time of the millennium, the time of the golden age ╞the utopia that people have been looking to. It is finally ushered in. The time of the millennium is almost like a return to the days of the Garden of Eden before the fall. Why? It is because those who have rebelled against God have been destroyed. The antichrist and the false prophet have been cast into the lake of fire, and Satan has been bound and sealed in the bottomless pit. Also, those nations that are removed into the millennium will be ruled with a rod of iron. If there is any rebellion, it will be punished right away. The Lord shall rule over this earth with those who shall reign with Him. The nation of Israel shall be a nation of priests, as God had promised to Abraham and Moses. They shall be a nation of priests who go out and teach the nations to serve the Lord. We will have the best environment the world has ever known.

At the end of the millennium, Satan will be released temporarily and will tempt the world. After the millennium, there will be a great multitude following him in the last rebellion. You know, dear brothers and sisters, we often think people are bad because we do not have a good environment or if our environment is changed, we will be changed. But this is not so. Why? During the millennium, you will have the best environment that can be had, and yet, hearts will not be changed. The basic problem is not a matter of the environment; it is a matter of the heart. Even the submission which you will find during the millennium time will be an outward thing, not an inward reality. Those born during those years will have never known the corruption nor the violence which we have known today. That is the reason they will be tested before they will be allowed to be removed to the new heaven and the new earth.

It is here that we find the last rebellion. Gog and Magog will come up and surround the camp of the saints and the holy city, but they will be consumed by fire. We know from history that Gog and Magog were a nomadic, cruel people who traditionally hated God's people. In Ezekiel 38 and 39, we find Gog and Magog will be the last and final enemy of the nation of Israel before the millennium. Probably, they were the northern confederacy; but here, it is after the millennium, therefore, Gog and Magog are used symbolically. It is not limited to any geographical area or any ethnic people; but it represents those who hate God's people. Probably, they are jealous, jealous of the grace of God which He has shown to those who reign with Christ. They are also jealous of the nation of Israel because God's grace is upon them. Because of all this jealousy, there will be the last rebellion. But thank God, they will be consumed with fire.

Now after such things have happened, John said, "I saw." What did John begin to see? He saw the great white throne and Him that sat on it. Dear brothers and sisters, this is not the throne of grace that we approach today. In Hebrews, we find:

Let us approach therefore with boldness to the throne of grace, that we may receive mercy, and find grace for seasonable help. (Hebrews 4:16)

The throne of God to us today is a throne of grace because of the blood of our Lord Jesus; because He has opened a new and living way for us; because He is our great high priest. Therefore, it is with boldness that we approach the throne of grace to receive mercy and find grace for every need.

However, one day, the door of grace will be closed and the great white throne will be set. It is a throne of eternal judgment. God is going to judge all men. It is a great throne, a great white throne. The very size of that throne gives you the impression of God's authority, greatness and power.

How will He judge all men? In Hebrews, we are told, "It is the portion of men once to die, and after this judgment." So here you will find all men will be judged at the great white throne. It is called a white throne. Why? It is because white speaks of purity. In other words, before that throne, every man will be judged with no partiality, no prejudice and with absolute justice. How terrible must be that great white throne. It is the last act of time because, after the great white throne judgment, time will pass away and eternity will return.

"And there is One who sits upon that throne." Now who is that One? In John 5:22, the Lord Jesus said, "Neither does the Father judge anyone but has given all judgment to the Son." In other words, the One who sits upon that great white throne is none other than our Lord Jesus. He sits upon that throne and to Him has been entrusted the judgment of all men. You remember when Peter was in the house of Cornelius, he said:

And he commanded us to preach to the people, and to testify that he [the Lord Jesus] it is who was determinately appointed of God to be judge of living and dead. (Acts 10:42)

Also, when Paul spoke in Athens to the Athenians, he said:

God has set a day in which he is going to judge the habitable earth in righteousness by the man whom he has appointed. (Acts 17:31)

The One whom God has appointed to judge the whole world is none other than our Lord Jesus. While He was on earth, He was judged by man, but now it is His turn to judge all men.

"From whose face the earth and the heaven fled, and place was not found for them." You remember when our Lord Jesus was crucified on the cross how the sun hid its face, but here even the heaven and the earth will pass away before the face of our Lord Jesus. They cannot stand to see His face. The whole earth and heaven will be consumed; all the elements will be burned and consumed. Nothing can stand before His face. What a terrible day it must be, to think that people have to face Him, the One whom the heaven and earth cannot face.

"And I saw the dead, great and small, standing before the throne." It is the judgment of the dead; the living have already been judged. All those who have died will be raised to be judged. In John 5:28-29, the Lord Jesus told us:

Wonder not at this, for an hour is coming in which all who are in the tombs shall hear his voice, and shall go forth; those that have practiced good, to resurrection of life, and those that have done evil, to resurrection of judgment.

We know that the resurrection of the just happened before the millennium, one thousand years before. Now this is the time of the resurrection of the evil and all those who are evil shall come into judgment. Dear brothers and sisters, how we thank the Lord that even though we are no good, yet because we have trusted in the Lord Jesus, God has counted us as righteous. Again, in John 5:24, the Lord Jesus said:

Verily, verily, I say unto you, that he that hears my word, and believes him that has sent me, has life eternal, and does not come into judgment, but is passed out of death into life.

It is because of His shed blood, because of the life that is given to us, that God has counted us as righteous. We will not enter into this judgment of the great white throne. We have passed out of death into life. Oh dear brothers and sisters, by grace we who have believed in the Lord Jesus have been delivered from this great white throne judgment. We will not be there because Christ has already been judged for us on Calvary's cross. Those who do not receive Him, who reject the Son, who do not accept His mercy and grace shall be resurrected and enter into this judgment. No one can escape! The sea will give up its dead. Death and hades will give up their dead. Everyone who has rejected the Son, everyone who has despised the love of God, everyone who has refused to accept the Lord Jesus as his Savior will be at the great white throne. How will they be judged?

"And books were opened." These books are the personal files recorded of every man. You know, God keeps a record. He has a file of every man from the time he is born to the time he dies. Everything is in the book: every word you have spoken, good or idle; every thought you have thought, good or evil; every action you have taken, good or bad; every attitude you maintain, good or bad; every relationship you have, good or bad. Everything in your life, to the minutest detail, is in the book. There is nothing lost. Your whole life is filed in God's record.

You know, people are rather frightened today. I often read in the paper how the government, the F.B.I. or C.I.A. or whatever it may be, seems to keep a file on everybody and they seem to know anything and everything you have done; but don't be afraid of that because they miss a lot. But there is one book of which you really need to be afraid because nothing is missed; everything is there. Does God really keep such a record? He does. How does He keep it? Where does He keep His file cabinet? Can it be destroyed?

Let me tell you a story that D.L. Moody, the great evangelist, told about himself when he was a boy. Once when he was in a river or lake, he was drowning. When he went down under the surface, in a split second, he saw his whole life projected as on a screen right before his eyes. Just in a second, he saw his whole life. So Moody said the books that God keeps are your memory.

God keeps that book in your memory. Everything is written there and, when the time comes, God just brings it forth and, in your memory, your whole life will come before you in a second. Everything you have done in your life you will see right before you. That is probably the way God keeps His records.

Dear brothers and sisters, isn't it terrifying to see your whole life projected before you, not only for you to see, not only for God to see, not only for the Lord to see but for all these billions and billions, even countless, people to see? Your whole life is an opened book. Everybody will see it. Does God need to judge anyone? He doesn't need to judge anyone, you judge yourself.

Before C.H. Spurgeon believed in the Lord Jesus, he was seeking and was burdened with his sin. He was seeking for salvation and said, "If God is righteous, then God must condemn me to eternal death; because if He does not condemn me to eternal death, He is not righteous."

There is no need for God to condemn anybody; you will condemn yourself when you see what you have done, when you see your whole life projected before you. There will be no argument before the great white throne. There will be no excuse given for anything. Nobody can give any excuse. When you see your whole life projected before you, you hang down your head and say: "God is just. He is just. I deserve eternal death. He is right." Everybody will give righteousness to God. TERRIFYING!!!

But dear brothers and sisters, how we thank the Lord for the precious blood of the Lamb. When the blood cleanses, it washes it away. It is no longer there. Even God will not see it anymore. Thank God for that!

Brothers and sisters, do we realize what we have received? Do we realize the grace, the mercy, the love, the salvation which we have received? In the light of the great white throne, how we need to thank the Lord Jesus for what He has done for us, what love He has given to us.

"And another book was opened which is that of life." Against all these books that pile high at the great white throne there is another book, and that book is called the book of life. Anyone whose name is not written in the book of life shall be judged by the books. In other words, if your name is written in the book of life, you will not be judged by the books. Who could pass that judgment? To be judged by the books means you will be judged according to the works which you have done. The letter to the Romans and the letter to the Galatians have proved to us that no one can be justified by works. We are justified by faith, not by works, by faith in the Lord Jesus. At the great white throne everyone will be judged according to works, but who can be justified? Nobody! No one can be justified by works, now or forever.

How we need to thank God that our names are written in the book of life. You remember in Luke 10, when the Lord sent the seventy out, they came back rejoicing and said: "Now even the evil spirits are subjected to us. See what power we have." They were so happy with such manifestations of divine power. You know what the Lord said? "Rejoice not because the evil spirits are subject to you but rejoice because your names are written in the book of life in heaven." To cast out evil spirits is to demonstrate the powers of the age to come; but to have your name written in the book of life is eternal!

IT IS ETERNAL! Brothers and sisters, you need to rejoice that, by God's grace, not by your works, not because you are good, your name is written in the Lamb's book of life. Thank God! Your name is written in the book of life. MAKE SURE OF THAT! If you are not sure whether your name is written in the book of the Lamb, make sure of it today. If you don't, it may be too late. If your name isn't found there, then you will be judged according to the books.

How can your name be written in the Lamb's book of life? It is by trusting in the Lamb of God who takes away the sin of the world, by believing in the Lord Jesus; then your name will be written in the book of life. Then rejoice over this fact.

Furthermore, in Philippians 4:3, Paul, when talking about his fellow-workers, said:

Yea, I ask thee also, true yokefellow, assist them, who have contended along with me in the glad tidings, with Clement also, and my other fellow-labourers, whose names are in the book of life.

Isn't that wonderful? How can we serve God if our names are not written in the book of life? In other words, service comes out of life. Because our names are written in the book of life, therefore, our service will be accepted by God. If our names are not written in the book of life, no matter how you serve, your service will be rejected. God does not want your service because the more you serve, the more you do a disservice to Him. But if your name is written in the book of life, then dear brothers and sisters, it is time you start to serve Him. You serve Him with the life He has given to you.

Another thing to remember: to have your name written in the book of life is a protection. Why? If you read Revelation 13 and 17, you will see that those whose names are written in the book of life will not worship the beast; but those whose names are not written in the book of life will worship the beast. In other words, with your name written in the book of life, it will keep you away from sin and evil. Thank God for that!

Thank God that your names are written in the book of life. How important it is!

Why is that book of life there at the great white throne? We say it is the judgment of the dead. Those who believe in the Lord Jesus have been resurrected one thousand years ahead of them and will never come unto the great white throne. Why should the book of life be there? Is it just to serve as a check lest anyone's name may be there and he may be judged? Certainly, it will be more than that, but I don't know because the Bible is silent. There is only one explanation which I may offer. Now you can take it or leave it because it is not in the Bible. I think, probably, the book of life is there because of those who may die during the millennium years. You remember in Isaiah 65:20, it says:

And the sinner being a hundred years old shall be accursed.

Maybe there are people who are born during the millennium and die at that time. It may be some of them have their names in the book of life. I don't know; but there may be such an explanation. Anyway, at the last judgment, all whose names are not written in the book of life will be judged according to the books, according to the work they have done in their life, and the result will be that they will be cast into the lake of fire, which is the second death. Remember, the lake of fire, or hell, as people usually say, is not made for man. Hell is prepared for Satan. Satan is cast into the lake of fire, but those who follow him have to keep company with him. That is why you will find those who are judged and condemned will be cast into the lake of fire. That will be the end of time and, thank God, after that, comes eternity.

Therefore, dear brothers and sisters, we need to see the Lord Jesus in the light of the great white throne. Today, He offers His grace to us, but one day, He will sit on that throne and judge all men. In what way do you want to see Him? Do you want to see Him as the Lamb of God who takes away the sin of the world, as the burnt offering, willingly offered to the Father on behalf of the world? Or do want to see Him as the judge on the great white throne?

We, who have believed in Him, have much to thank Him for, so may the Lord help us.

Our Heavenly Father, we do praise and thank Thee because the One whom Thou hast appointed to judge the living and the dead is the very One whom Thou hast sent into the world to save the lost. Oh, how we praise and thank Thee that Thou hast opened our eyes to see Him as the Lamb of God. How we praise and thank Thee for faith given in believing and trusting in Him. How we thank Thee that our names are, by grace, written in the book of life. Oh, how we thank Thee for the salvation and for the favor that Thou hast given to us.

Oh, how it is our prayer and our longing that many more may come to know Thee in this way because it is Thy will that all shall be saved and come to the knowledge of God. Thou dost not want anyone to perish. Oh, Lord, we pray and ask Thee, since Thou hast saved us, may Thy compassion fill our hearts that we may go out and seek and find the lost. Oh, that the gospel of Jesus Christ may be preached. Oh, that many more may be brought into Thy kingdom. We pray for our friends. We pray for our relatives. We pray for our neighbors. We pray for those with whom we come in contact. Oh, we do pray, Lord, open their eyes that they may see Thee as the Lamb of God who takes away the sin of the world. Oh, we pray that they may not reject Thee and then, one day, stand before that great white throne. How can they face Thy face? Oh, Lord, have mercy, have mercy. We ask in Thy precious Name. Amen.

VISION OF THE NEW JERUSALEM

Revelation 21:1-7 And I saw a new heaven and a new earth; for the first heaven and the first earth had passed away, and the sea exists no more. And I saw the holy city, new Jerusalem, coming down out of the heaven from God, prepared as a bride adorned for her husband. And I heard a loud voice out of the heaven, saying, Behold, the tabernacle of God is with men, and he shall tabernacle with them, and they shall be his people, and God himself shall be with them, their God. And he shall wipe away every tear from their eyes; and death shall not exist anymore, nor grief, nor cry, nor distress shall exist anymore, for the former things have passed away. And he that sat on the throne said, Behold, I make all things new. And he says to me, Write, for these words are true and faithful. And he said to me, It is done. I am the Alpha and the Omega, the beginning and the end. I will give to him that thirsts of the fountain of the water of life freely. He that overcomes shall inherit these things, and I will be to him God, and he shall be to me son.

Revelation 22:1-5 And he shewed me a river of water of life, bright as crystal, going out of the throne of God and of the Lamb. In the midst of its street, and of the river, on this side and on that side, the tree of life, producing twelve fruits, in each month yielding its fruit; and the leaves of the tree for healing of the nations. And no curse shall be any more; and the throne of God and of the Lamb shall be in it; and his servants shall serve him, and they shall see his face; and his name is on their foreheads. And night shall not be any more, and no need of a lamp, and light of the sun; for the Lord God shall shine upon them, and they shall reign to the ages of ages.

We have been considering this book of Revelation. We believe that God wants us to see His Son, our Lord Jesus Christ, in relation to our time, that is, to see the Lord Jesus in the light of the end days. For this, we find a series of seven visions of our Lord Jesus being given. Now we come to the last of the seven visions. It is the consummation of all the visions that have gone before because, in this vision, we shall see the fulfillment of the eternal purpose of God and the manifestation of eternal reality.

Here John said, "I saw." Now what did he see? He saw the holy city, new Jerusalem, coming down out of the heaven from God prepared as a bride adorned for her husband. What is the meaning of "the holy city, new Jerusalem"? It is explained in verse 3:

Behold, the tabernacle of God is with men and He shall tabernacle with them.

This holy city, new Jerusalem, is the tabernacle of God with man. We know that, from the very beginning, it has been the will of God that He should tabernacle with men. It was for this reason that He created man in the first place. After man was created, He put him in the Garden and talked with him; but God's purpose is more than that. God desires not only to have an external communication with man whom He created but God's desire is that man might eat the tree of life, that is to say, that man might receive His life and come into union with Him, and thereby have an inward relationship of life and an inner communion with God. In other words, God desires to dwell among men. The word dwell probably can be better expressed by the use of the word abide. It is the will of God that He abide with and in man so that man may abide in God. We know the word abide simply means "to make home." God desires to make His home in man and with man; thus man may find in God his eternal home. It was the original thought of God to tabernacle, to dwell, to abide in and with man; but unfortunately, man failed because he rebelled against God's command. The will of God was frustrated; the plan of God was delayed; but the purpose of God never changed and, because of that we find in the Scriptures how God began to work. As our Lord Jesus said:

My Father worketh hitherto and I work. (John 5:17)

First, He delivered a nation, Israel, out of Egypt. He brought them to Himself and, at Mount Sinai, He gave them not only the law but the tabernacle. God expressed His desire to His redeemed people, Israel, saying, "I want to dwell among you and for this reason build Me a tabernacle." God could dwell among His people, Israel, through the tabernacle and, of course, we know primarily that tabernacle represents our Lord Jesus. How can God dwell among men except through our Lord Jesus? Secondarily, the tabernacle represents the church. It is because of the redemptive work of our Lord Jesus that a new tabernacle, a new body is being raised. Then our Lord Jesus came to this earth, and it says in John 1:14:

And the Word became flesh, and dwelt among us (and we have contemplated his glory, a glory as of an only begotten with a father), full of grace and truth.

When our Lord Jesus was on earth, He was the tabernacle of God. Through Him, God tabernacled among men; but after His death and resurrection, He received a new body, a corporate body, the body of Christ, the church. From that day until now, the church of God is the tabernacle of God among men. God is able to present Himself to mankind through the church and He is to be seen, to be heard through the church. This is what the church is, the tabernacle of God with man.

Thank God, in the final stage, we will find the tabernacle of God is the holy city, the New Jerusalem. The holy city, the New Jerusalem, is the consummation and the gathering up of all the works of God through the Old and New Testaments. The composite of Old Testament saints and New Testament saints will become the holy city, the New Jerusalem. This will become the tabernacle of God with man and this will be the permanent, eternal tabernacle of God with man. God will dwell with man on the new earth through that tabernacle, and it will continue on for eternity.

John said, "I saw the holy city." This holy city is the wife of the Lamb. How can a city be a wife? Certainly, you cannot take this in the literal sense; you have to take it in the spiritual sense. What is a city? What does a city represent? A city speaks of a unity, many, yet one. In the city, you find many people; yet these many people become one city, one unity. Also, a city is where the government is; therefore, when you speak of a city, it reminds you of a government. There is a government and only one government over that city. A city speaks of order, and in this city there is order. It is not something disorganized, disintegrated or scattered but this city is of divine order. Then, of course, there is development there. Therefore, in the final consummation, God will have a city which is a unity, a oneness, under the government of His Son because "the government shall be upon His shoulder" (Isaiah 9:6).

Also, a city depicts separation and protection. It is separated, yet it is protected. It is called a holy city. You know, the word holy simply means "set apart." It is in opposition to being common. It is not something for every purpose, but it is set apart for one purpose only, for the Lord, the wife of the Lamb and nothing else.

It is called the new Jerusalem. As the Jerusalem of old was to the nation of Israel, so this new Jerusalem is to us. Jerusalem means "peace"; but strange to say, this peace does not come easily. It has to go through many conflicts, many battles, many controversies, many travails;

but finally, when the Prince of Peace shall return, there will be peace in Jerusalem. Also, we are exhorted to pray for the peace of that city. Dear brothers and sisters, this is what the new Jerusalem will be, a city of peace. Yet it is not the peace that comes by compromise or negotiation, which is never lasting; but it is a peace which comes by purity and righteousness. When the Prince of Peace shall rule over this earth, then you will find He will rule through this city, the new Jerusalem. He shall reign in that city, and through it, He shall reign over the whole earth.

Jerusalem is the center of the national life of the people of Israel. We find it is said in the Psalms that the twelve tribes will flow together to Jerusalem to worship the Lord; therefore, Jerusalem is the very center of the life together of the twelve tribes of Israel. Dear brothers and sisters, this is what the new Jerusalem will be to us, the center of our living together. We will no longer be scattered, but together, and centered upon the Lord, who is the very center of that city.

The temple was in Jerusalem; the throne was in Jerusalem. The temple of God was built on Mount Moriah, and the throne of David was set up on Mount Zion. Jerusalem is built on these two mounts; so there you have the temple and the throne. In Jerusalem, there is worship, there is dominion, there is authority; so in this new Jerusalem, we find the same thing. The throne of God and of the Lamb shall be set in the center of that city. There will be no temple in that city. Why? It is because the whole city is the temple. There His people shall worship Him. There His people shall serve Him. There His people shall reign as kings forever and ever.

Here you will find, at the very last, the holy city, the new Jerusalem coming down out of heaven. Everything is ready, and this is the wife of the Lamb.

In a very real sense, when you look at this city, you will find it is nothing but a corporate expression of Christ. In that city, Christ is indeed all and in all. There is nothing but Christ, and yet it is Christ being all in all to us all. We know this is the purpose of God: that Christ may be all and in all.

Now just look at this city for a moment. When John saw that city coming down out of heaven, he just saw it outwardly; then gradually, he was led into the city, even into the center of it. Whatever he saw outwardly was but the inward manifestation of what was in the center of that city. First of all, he saw the outward appearance: the city descending down from heaven with the shining of God. In that city, there is no need for the sun or the moon. Why? God Himself, the Lamb is the lamp thereof. God is the light and the Lamb is the lamp thereof. In other words, God enlightens that city.

But there is another point we have to remember: Why is it that John saw the shining of God in that city? It is because all the materials of that city are transparent. Even the gold is transparent gold. Now we have never see any gold that is transparent because there is always the impurity; but one day, you will find the gold there is transparent like crystal. You can see through it.

The wall is made of jasper, precious stone, blue in color; yet it is crystal-like jasper. You have never seen a crystal which is like jasper because, today, there is so much impurity; but one day, there will be the wall made of crystal-like jasper. In other words, not only do the materials represent Christ but there is no shadow, no shade. It is all crystal-like, all transparent, no spot, no wrinkle. When the light of God shines through these metals, through these stones, through these things, it just simply shines right on through with no resistance, no detraction, no deflection. The light is able to shine right through the whole city. The whole city is so transparent that the light of God just shines through it, and not only through it, but magnified by it. The reflection of light in that city is tremendous, and this is why John saw the city as the shining of God.

Dear brothers and sisters, is it not the will of God that He should be magnified and manifested through us, His people? Today, though, no matter how much Christ is being reflected by us, we deflect Him. Somehow, there is a resistance in us somewhere. In other words, there is always impurity within us. There is always some shadow, some shade, some resistance, some spot, some wrinkle.

We are opaque, we are not transparent! Sometimes, we cry out and say, "O Lord, why is it people do not see Thee as Thou art?" It is because they see more of us than of Christ. They may see some of Christ; but even that "some of Christ" is being twisted. Why? It is because we are so impure; there is so much spot and wrinkle in us.

Thank God the Holy Spirit is working towards the end; and when that end shall arrive, truly the church shall be a glorious church without spot or wrinkle or any such thing; but it will be holy and without blemish. One day, you will find Christ is so incorporated, so organized, so wrought into our life that it is nothing but Christ. There will be no more resistance. On the one hand, it is we; yet on the other hand, it is Christ all and in all.

Not only will the light of God be there but the light of God will be magnified by that city; therefore, John saw the shining of God. It is by that light, the light of the city, that the nations walk before God. In other words, the light of God enlightens that city, and the light of the city enlightens the nations. It is in that light the nations shall walk, resulting in their bringing worship to God. It is true, "If we walk in the light, as He is in the light, we shall have fellowship with one another and the blood of Jesus Christ, God's Son, cleanses us from all our sin"; but on the other hand, if we walk in the light, we shall be the light of the world. The world shall walk in our light; but if we do not walk in the light, then how can we enlighten the world or how can the world walk in the light and come to worship God?

It is here at the consummation of time when eternity shall begin. The work of God is complete. The work of transformation is fulfilled. Brothers and sisters, what is the work of the Holy Spirit today? The work of the Holy Spirit is predominantly and mainly the work of transformation. He is transforming us from glory to glory, according to the image of God's Son; but one day, the transformation shall be completed, the consummation shall be perfect; and this is the holy city, the new Jerusalem. Thank God, it is not left for us to complete or we would never make it; but thank God, this is the work of the Holy Spirit. God has entrusted His work to His own Spirit and the Holy Spirit shall complete it. The day shall come when the Old Testament saints and the New Testament saints, the redemptive work of God throughout the ages, shall be consummated in that holy city and God shall be magnified, the shining of God!

Then John took a closer look to see the wall and the foundations. The wall was made of crystal-like jasper. Jasper is blue in color, and blue is a heavenly color. In Revelation 4, we find the One who sits upon the throne looks like a jasper stone. In other words, this jasper stone speaks of God's own nature, how heavenly He is, and yet it is crystal-like. We shall be heavenly, there will be nothing earthly; it shall be crystal-like.

The wall is of tremendous height, one hundred and forty-four cubits (one cubit is an arm's length to your middle finger). We have never seen a city wall as high as this one. Why is it so high? It is because it is so separated, so well-protected. Dear brothers and sisters, we know in the very beginning after God planted the garden of Eden (which means the garden of pleasure), everything was so pleasant in the garden; yet because there was no wall the enemy slipped in and tempted man. Thank God, in eternity to come, you will find a holy city, and it is a garden. How do we know this? The tree of life is everywhere, and yet the city is walled in. There is a tremendously high wall all around the city: well-protected. There will be no more danger of the enemy coming in: wholly separated.

Of course, brothers and sisters, we know separation is not just an external thing. Separation is the impartation, the incorporation of the life of God in us. The more the life of God is built up in us, the more we are separated and protected. In the final stage, we see the separation is complete; the protection is perfect: one hundred and forty-four cubits, the multiple of twelve, which is the number of eternal completeness.

Now let us see what is said about the foundations. We find they are made of twelve precious stones, every stone being different. These twelve foundations bear the names of the twelve apostles of Christ. Dear brothers and sisters, on the one hand, whatever precious stone it may be, whether jasper, emerald, or some other, it is nothing but the expression of Christ in different individuals.

IT IS CHRIST, yet it is CHRIST in Peter, CHRIST in James, CHRIST in John. In other words, our identity will never be lost. Do not think because it will be Christ all and in all, we will lose our identity. Not at all! You know, in this world if they try to make people the same, the one thing they try to do is make you lose your identity so that you become one of the parts of that whole. Dear brothers and sisters, God has something much better. On the one hand, it is Christ all and in all, it is neither you nor me, neither Jews nor Gentiles. Yet on the other hand, we never lose our identity. Peter is always Peter, to eternity. John is always John, to eternity. James is always James, to eternity. You are always you, to eternity.

Now don't copy anyone because, if you do, in eternity you will still be you, so you have lost your time. It's no use! Your identity will always be there. Brothers and sisters, our individualism must be dealt with by the cross; but the individuality always remains. Therefore, you will find the twelve stones bear the names of the twelve apostles of the Lamb, and every stone is different. It is Christ; but the way Christ is organizing Peter is very different from the way Christ is organizing John. John expresses Christ in a unique way and Peter expresses Christ in a Petrine way and you should express Christ in your way. You are not expressing you and I am not expressing me, but we are all expressing Christ; and it takes all of us to express Him as all and in all.

The twelve gates bear the names of the twelve tribes of Israel. Why? It is because salvation comes from the Jews. In the beginning, God called Abraham and, from Abraham, the nation of Israel; and the Savior is to come from that nation. It is twelve pearls, and they speak of the work of the Holy Spirit. Oh, how the Holy Spirit works, even though He was not present in the Old Testament times. He came to be on this earth only after our Lord Jesus was glorified; yet we see, in the Old Testament, it was the work of the Holy Spirit. It is through His work throughout the ages that you find here both Israel and the church, all the redeemed of the Lord being gathered together into that holy city to be the wife of the Lamb.

Look a little closer as you enter into the city and you find a street there made of pure gold, transparent as glass. Again, we have never seen such gold; you don't have it on earth. Now gold speaks of the nature of God. What is a street? Street in the Scripture always speaks of "fellowship" because if you want to go anywhere, you have to walk on the street. Dear brothers and sisters, on this earth, there are too many streets: dead-end streets and one-way streets. So here, you are all confused, all confused, but dear brothers and sisters, one day, there will be only one street and that street will lead you to the throne and nowhere else. You will never get lost and never come to a dead end.

Here the fellowship of the saints is on the basis of the divine life of God, this is the street. Oh, how sad it is that people today do not maintain that fellowship on the ground of Christ. Instead, they try to maintain it on certain doctrines, certain forms, certain systems, ways or methods. Brothers and sisters, all these are byways and highways that lead to dead ends. There is only one street and that street, that fellowship, is on gold, pure gold, transparent! In other words, our fellowship is based on the life of God in Christ and nothing else.

Also, our fellowship shall be so open; it is transparent. Today, even though we do fellowship, we sometimes feel we have to hide something. Sometimes, you think if you are too open, you will be misunderstood; people will look down on you. But dear brothers and sisters, if our fellowship is purely on the ground of Christ, it can be transparent, as transparent gold. It is the fellowship of the life of Christ, one with another, and this fellowship will lead us to the throne, will lead us to God. It will not lead us astray, away from God, but it will lead us to God and to worship.

There is only one street and one river of life. This river of life comes from the throne of God and of the Lamb and it goes through the whole city and wherever the river of life goes, the tree of life grows. It grows in the middle of the river; it grows on the two sides of the river. The tree of life is everywhere! The river of life and the tree of life growing everywhere speak of life abundant. In other words, in that city, it is nothing but the life of God. The life of God flows and overflows. THANK GOD! As our Lord Jesus said: "I come that you might have life and have it more abundantly." Oh, how this is fully realized. It is life! How much of our fellowship today is life? But one day, it will be life, it will be life abundant! Everywhere you see life. There is no more death, no more tears, no more pain, no more distress! All these things have passed away.

Even the sun and moon are not needed in that city. We need the sun and the moon today. If the sun should be completely wiped out or destroyed, within seconds, we would all be frozen. We need all these things as they make us live. They are absolute necessities; but one day, we shall find in Christ all our need. We will be delivered even from the need of the sun or moon. Think of that!

How much are we delivered from these physical things today? It is true, the Lord is delivering us; but there are still many physical things which are absolute necessities. However, the day is coming when we shall have no need of them because we will find Christ our all and in all. HE will be our sun. HE will be our moon. HE will be our light. HE will be our everything. OH! THANK GOD FOR THAT DAY! What deliverance it will be. We will not lean upon anything physical anymore. God will be everything to us.

Then you go to the very center of that city and there is the explanation, the meaning. In the center, you find the throne of God and of the Lamb. One day, the throne of God and of the Lamb shall be eternally set up in the city of God and, through that city, He shall reign over the new heaven and the new earth. All who are in the city are kings. They shall reign with God and with Christ eternally. They shall have the name of God upon their foreheads and shall serve Him as servants forever.

What do we see here? We see Christ all and in all. We see God all and in all. We see Christ in the center in the midst of the city. We see the city as a corporate expression of God and of His Christ through eternity.

Dear brothers and sisters, this is the realization of the eternal purpose of God. God said:

Write, for these words are true and faithful. It is done. I am the Alpha and the Omega, the beginning and the end.

So dear brothers and sisters, we have such a blessed hope before us. Oh! How we need to look forward to that day. Sometimes, when we look around, we begin to wonder; sometimes, when we look at ourselves, we are disappointed; but let's look up and see that God is going to get what He wants. Christ shall be all and in all and we shall be His eternal home and, through us, He shall tabernacle among men!

Our Heavenly Father, our hearts do rejoice in Thy presence, knowing that Thou art God. Thou art the God who works even now until Thy purpose is fulfilled. Oh, how we praise and thank Thee that it is Thy will that Christ shall be all and in all, and it shall be. Oh, we do pray that, even today, we may learn something of that nature that we do not need to postpone and delay Thy working but, in a way, we may speed up Thy work by yielding and cooperating with Thee. How we long that Christ may truly be all and in all to us, individually and together; and we look forward to that day when the shining of God shall become the shining of that city and nations shall walk in the light thereof. To Thee be all the praise and glory. In the Name of our Lord Jesus. Amen.

Other Books Printed By
Christian Testimony Ministry

SPEAKER	TITLE
DANA CONGDON	MARRIAGE, SINGLENESS, AND THE WILL OF GOD
	RECOVERY & RESTORATION
	THE HOLY SPIRIT
	HEBREWS
A.J. FLACK	TENT OF HIS SPLENDOUR
STEPHEN KAUNG	ACTS
	BE YE THEREFORE PERFECT
	CALLED OUT UNTO CHRIST
	CALLED TO THE FELLOWSHIP OF GOD'S SON
	DIVINE LIFE AND ORDER
	FOR ME TO LIVE IS CHRIST
	GLORIOUS LIBERTY OF THE CHILDREN OF GOD
	GOD'S PURPOSE FOR THE FAMILY
	I WILL BUILD MY CHURCH
	MEDITATIONS ON THE KINGDOM
	RECOVERY
	SPIRITUAL EXERCISE
	SPIRITUAL LIFE (II CORINTHIANS SERIES)
	TEACH US TO PRAY
	THE CROSS
	THE FULNESS OF CHRIST—IN THE BOOK OF REVELATION
	THE HEADSHIP OF CHRIST
	THE KINGDOM AND THE CHURCH
	THE KINGDOM OF GOD
	THE LAST CALL TO THE CHURCHES, THE CALL TO OVERCOME
	THE LIFE OF OUR LORD JESUS
	THE LIFE OF THE CHURCH, THE BODY OF CHRIST
	THE LORD'S TABLE
	TWO GUIDEPOSTS FOR INHERITING THE KINGDOM
	VISION OF CHRIST (REVELATION)
	WHO ARE WE?

WHY DO WE SO GATHER?
WORSHIP

LANCE LAMBERT   CALLED UNTO HIS ETERNAL GLORY
                      GOD'S ETERNAL PURPOSE
                      IN THE DAY OF THY POWER
                      JACOB I HAVE LOVED
                      LIVING FAITH
                      LESSONS FROM THE LIFE OF MOSES
                      LOVE DIVINE
                      MY HOUSE SHALL BE A HOUSE OF PRAYER
                      PREPARATION FOR THE COMING OF THE LORD
                      REIGNING WITH CHRIST
                      SPIRITUAL CHARACTER
                      THE GOSPEL OF THE KINGDOM
                      THE IMPORTANCE OF COVERING
                      THE LAST DAYS AND GOD'S PRIORITIES
                      THE PRIZE
                      THE SUPREMACY OF JESUS CHRIST
                      THINE IS THE POWER!
                      THOU ART MINE

T. AUSTIN-SPARKS   THE LORD'S TESTIMONY AND THE WORLD NEED

HARVEY CEDARS CONFERENCE

STEPHEN KAUNG   HEAVENLY VISION
                      SPIRITUAL RESPONSIBILITY

CONGDON, HILE, KAUNG SPIRITUAL MINISTRY
                      SPIRITUAL AUTHORITY
                      SPIRITUAL HOUSE
                      SPIRITUAL SUBMISSION

STEPHEN KAUNG   SPIRITUAL KNOWLEDGE
                      SPIRITUAL POWER
                      SPIRITUAL REALITY
                      SPIRITUAL VALUE
                      SPIRITUAL BLESSING
                      SPIRITUAL DISCERNMENT

www.ingramcontent.com/pod-product-compliance
Lightning Source LLC
Chambersburg PA
CBHW051042030426

42339CB00006B/147